NEW AND

SELECTED

POEMS

OTHER BOOKS BY MARY OLIVER

House of Light

Dream Work

American Primitive

Twelve Moons

The River Styx, Ohio and Other Poems

No Voyage and Other Poems

CHAPBOOKS

Sleeping in the Forest

The Night Traveler

NEW AND SELECTED POEMS

Mary Oliver

BEACON PRESS

BOSTON

Beacon Press
25 Beacon Street
Boston, Massachusetts 02108-2892

Beacon Press books
are published under the auspices of
the Unitarian Universalist Association of Congregations.

00   99   98   97   96   14   13   12   11   10

Text design by Dede Cummings/Irving Perkins Associates

Library of Congress Cataloging-in-Publication Data

Oliver, Mary, 1935–
[Poems. Selections]
New and selected poems / Mary Oliver.
p.   cm.
ISBN 0-8070-6818-7 (cloth)
ISBN 0-8070-6819-5 (paper)
I. Title.
PS3565.L5N47   1992
811′.54 — dc20   92-7767

Copyright page continues on page 258.

For

Molly Malone Cook

CONTENTS

New Poems
(1991–1992)

FROM *House of Light*
(1990)

FROM *Twelve Moons*

(1979)

FROM *The Night Traveler*

(1978)

AND *Sleeping in the Forest*

(1978)

AND FIVE POEMS

NOT PREVIOUSLY INCLUDED

IN ANY VOLUME

FROM *The River Styx, Ohio*

and Other Poems

(1972)

FROM *No Voyage*
and Other Poems
(1963 and 1965)

NEW
POEMS

———— ❦ ————

(1 9 9 1 – 1 9 9 2)

Rain

1

All afternoon it rained, then
such power came down from the clouds
on a yellow thread,
as authoritative as God is supposed to be.
When it hit the tree, her body
opened forever.

2 The Swamp

Last night, in the rain, some of the men climbed over
    the barbed-wire fence of the detention center.
In the darkness they wondered if they could do it, and knew
    they had to try to do it.
In the darkness they climbed the wire, handful after handful
    of barbed wire.
Even in the darkness most of them were caught and sent back
    to the camp inside.
But a few are still climbing the barbed wire, or wading through
    the blue swamp on the other side.

What does barbed wire feel like when you grip it, as though
    it were a loaf of bread, or a pair of shoes?
What does barbed wire feel like when you grip it, as though
    it were a plate and a fork, or a handful of flowers?
What does barbed wire feel like when you grip it, as though
    it were the handle of a door, working papers, a clean sheet
    you want to draw over your body?

3

Or this one: on a rainy day, my uncle
lying in the flower bed,
cold and broken,
dragged from the idling car
with its plug of rags, and its gleaming
length of hose. My father
shouted,
then the ambulance came,
then we all looked at death,
then the ambulance took him away.
From the porch of the house
I turned back once again
looking for my father, who had lingered,
who was still standing in the flowers,
who was that motionless muddy man,
who was that tiny figure in the rain.

4 *Early Morning, My Birthday*

The snails on the pink sleds of their bodies are moving
    among the morning glories.
The spider is asleep among the red thumbs
    of the raspberries.
What shall I do, what shall I do?

The rain is slow.
The little birds are alive in it.
Even the beetles.
The green leaves lap it up.
What shall I do, what shall I do?

The wasp sits on the porch of her paper castle.
The blue heron floats out of the clouds.
The fish leap, all rainbow and mouth, from the dark water.

This morning the water lilies are no less lovely, I think,
    than the lilies of Monet.
And I do not want anymore to be useful, to be docile, to lead
children out of the fields into the text
of civility, to teach them that they are (they are not) better
    than the grass.

5 At the Edge of the Ocean

I have heard this music before,
saith the body.

6 The Garden

The kale's
puckered sleeve,
the pepper's
hollow bell,
the lacquered onion.

Beets, borage, tomatoes.
Green beans.

I came in and I put everything
on the counter: chives, parsley, dill,

the squash like a pale moon,
peas in their silky shoes, the dazzling
rain-drenched corn.

7 *The Forest*

At night
under the trees
the black snake
jellies forward
rubbing
roughly
the stems of the bloodroot,
the yellow leaves,
little boulders of bark,
to take off
the old life.
I don't know
if he knows
what is happening.
I don't know
if he knows
it will work.
In the distance
the moon and the stars
give a little light.
In the distance
the owl cries out.

In the distance
the owl cries out.
The snake knows
these are the owl's woods,

these are the woods of death,
these are the woods of hardship
where you crawl and crawl,
where you live in the husks of trees,
where you lie on the wild twigs
and they cannot bear your weight,
where life has no purpose
and is neither civil nor intelligent.

Where life has no purpose,
and is neither civil nor intelligent,
it begins
to rain,
it begins
to smell like the bodies
of flowers.
At the back of the neck
the old skin splits.
The snake shivers
but does not hesitate.
He inches forward.
He begins to bleed through
like satin.

Spring Azures

In spring the blue azures bow down
at the edges of shallow puddles
to drink the black rain water.
Then they rise and float away into the fields.

Sometimes the great bones of my life feel so heavy,
and all the tricks my body knows—
the opposable thumbs, the kneecaps,
and the mind clicking and clicking—

don't seem enough to carry me through this world
and I think: how I would like

to have wings—
blue ones—
ribbons of flame.

How I would like to open them, and rise
from the black rain water.

And then I think of Blake, in the dirt and sweat of London—a boy
staring through the window, when God came
fluttering up.

Of course, he screamed,
seeing the bobbin of God's blue body
leaning on the sill,
and the thousand-faceted eyes.

Well, who knows.
Who knows what hung, fluttering, at the window
between him and the darkness.

Anyway, Blake the hosier's son stood up
and turned away from the sooty sill and the dark city—
turned away forever
from the factories, the personal strivings,

to a life of the imagination.

When Death Comes

When death comes
like the hungry bear in autumn;
when death comes and takes all the bright coins from his purse

to buy me, and snaps the purse shut;
when death comes
like the measle-pox;

when death comes
like an iceberg between the shoulder blades,

I want to step through the door full of curiosity, wondering:
what is it going to be like, that cottage of darkness?

And therefore I look upon everything
as a brotherhood and a sisterhood,
and I look upon time as no more than an idea,
and I consider eternity as another possibility,

and I think of each life as a flower, as common
as a field daisy, and as singular,

and each name a comfortable music in the mouth,
tending, as all music does, toward silence,

and each body a lion of courage, and something
precious to the earth.

When it's over, I want to say: all my life
I was a bride married to amazement.
I was the bridegroom, taking the world into my arms.

When it's over, I don't want to wonder
if I have made of my life something particular, and real.
I don't want to find myself sighing and frightened,
or full of argument.

I don't want to end up simply having visited this world.

Picking Blueberries, Austerlitz, New York, 1957

Once, in summer,
   in the blueberries,
      I fell asleep, and woke
         when a deer stumbled against me.

I guess
   she was so busy with her own happiness
   she had grown careless
      and was just wandering along

listening
   to the wind as she leaned down
      to lip up the sweetness.
      So, there we were

with nothing between us
   but a few leaves, and the wind's
      glossy voice
         shouting instructions.

The deer
   backed away finally
      and flung up her white tail
         and went floating off toward the trees—

but the moment before she did that
   was so wide and so deep
      it has lasted to this day;
         I have only to think of her—

the flower of her amazement
    and the stalled breath of her curiosity,
        and even the damp touch of her solicitude
            before she took flight—

to be absent again from this world
    and alive, again, in another,
        for thirty years
            sleepy and amazed,

rising out of the rough weeds,
    listening and looking.
        Beautiful girl,
            where are you?

Her Grave

She would come back, dripping thick water, from the green bog.
She would fall at my feet, she would draw the black skin
from her gums, in a hideous and wonderful smile—
and I would rub my hands over her pricked ears and her
   cunning elbows,
and I would hug the barrel of her body, amazed at the unassuming
   perfect arch of her neck.

It took four of us to carry her into the woods.
We did not think of music,
but, anyway, it began to rain
slowly.

Her wolfish, invitational, half-pounce.

Her great and lordly satisfaction at having chased something.

My great and lordly satisfaction at her splash
of happiness as she barged
through the pitch pines swiping my face with her
wild, slightly mossy tongue.

Does the hummingbird think he himself invented his crimson throat?
He is wiser than that, I think.

A dog lives fifteen years, if you're lucky.

Do the cranes crying out in the high clouds
think it is all their own music?

A dog comes to you and lives with you in your own house, but you
do not therefore own her, as you do not own the rain, or the
trees, or the laws which pertain to them.

Does the bear wandering in the autumn up the side of the hill
think all by herself she has imagined the refuge and the refreshment
of her long slumber?

A dog can never tell you what she knows from the
smells of the world, but you know, watching her, that you know
almost nothing.

Does the water snake with his backbone of diamonds think
the black tunnel on the bank of the pond is a palace
of his own making?

She roved ahead of me through the fields, yet would come back, or
wait for me, or be somewhere.

Now she is buried under the pines.

Nor will I argue it, or pray for anything but modesty, and
not to be angry.

Through the trees there is the sound of the wind, palavering.

The smell of the pine needles, what is it but a taste
of the infallible energies?

How strong was her dark body!
How apt is her grave place.

How beautiful is her unshakable sleep.

Finally,
the slick mountains of love break
over us.

Goldenrod

On roadsides,
    in fall fields,
        in rumpy bunches,
            saffron and orange and pale gold,

in little towers,
    soft as mash,
        sneeze-bringers and seed-bearers,
            full of bees and yellow beads and perfect flowerlets

and orange butterflies.
    I don't suppose
        much notice comes of it, except for honey,
            and how it heartens the heart with its

blank blaze.
    I don't suppose anything loves it except, perhaps,
        the rocky voids
            filled by its dumb dazzle.

For myself,
    I was just passing by, when the wind flared
        and the blossoms rustled,
            and the glittering pandemonium

leaned on me.
    I was just minding my own business
        when I found myself on their straw hillsides,
            citron and butter-colored,

and was happy, and why not?
   Are not the difficult labors of our lives
      full of dark hours?
         And what has consciousness come to anyway, so far,

that is better than these light-filled bodies?
   All day
      on their airy backbones
         they toss in the wind,

they bend as though it was natural and godly to bend,
   they rise in a stiff sweetness,
      in the pure peace of giving
         one's gold away.

The Waterfall

FOR MAY SWENSON

For all they said,
   I could not see the waterfall
      until I came and saw the water falling,
         its lace legs and its womanly arms sheeting down,

while something howled like thunder,
   over the rocks,
      all day and all night—
         unspooling

like ribbons made of snow,
   or god's white hair.
      At any distance
         it fell without a break or seam, and slowly, a simple

preponderance—
   a fall of flowers—and truly it seemed
      surprised by the unexpected kindness of the air and
         light-hearted to be

flying at last.
   Gravity is a fact everybody
      knows about.
         It is always underfoot,

like a summons,
   gravel-backed and mossy,
      in every beetled basin—
         and imagination—

that striver,
    that third eye—
        can do a lot but
            hardly everything. The white, scrolled

wings of the tumbling water
    I never could have
        imagined. And maybe there will be,
           after all,

some slack and perfectly balanced
    blind and rough peace, finally,
        in the deep and green and utterly motionless pools after all that
           falling?

Peonies

This morning the green fists of the peonies are getting ready
    to break my heart
        as the sun rises,
            as the sun strokes them with his old, buttery fingers

and they open—
    pools of lace,
        white and pink—
            and all day the black ants climb over them,

boring their deep and mysterious holes
    into the curls,
        craving the sweet sap,
            taking it away

to their dark, underground cities—
    and all day
        under the shifty wind,
            as in a dance to the great wedding,

the flowers bend their bright bodies,
    and tip their fragrance to the air,
        and rise,
            their red stems holding

all that dampness and recklessness
    gladly and lightly,
        and there it is again—
            beauty the brave, the exemplary,

blazing open.
    Do you love this world?
        Do you cherish your humble and silky life?
            Do you adore the green grass, with its terror beneath?

Do you also hurry, half-dressed and barefoot, into the garden,
    and softly,
        and exclaiming of their dearness,
            fill your arms with the white and pink flowers,

with their honeyed heaviness, their lush trembling,
    their eagerness
        to be wild and perfect for a moment, before they are
        nothing, forever?

This Morning Again It Was in the Dusty Pines

Not in shyness but in disgust
the owl
turns its face from me and pours itself
into the air, hurrying

until it is out of sight—
and, after all,
even if we came by some miracle
upon a language which we both knew,

what is it I might say
there in the orange light of early morning,
in the owl's resting time,
that would have any pluck and worth in it?—

not admonition, or blame,
and not recrimination,
and not, I say, unholy weeping,
and not, for god's sake, any bending of the knees

in the cold and rough grass
under its gold and glassy eyes
which, in such a conversation, you must imagine
turned upon you.

So. I cannot improve upon the scene
as it happens:
my opportunity
and my stony silence

as death
rises up—
god's bark-colored thumb—
and opens the sheath of its wings

and turns its hungry, hooked head
upon me, and away,
and softly,
lamp-eyed,

becomes the perfect, billowing instrument
as it glides
through the wind
like a knife.

Marengo

Out of the sump rise the marigolds.
From the rim of the marsh, muslin with mosquitoes,
rises the egret, in his cloud-cloth.
Through the soft rain, like mist, and mica,
the withered acres of moss begin again.

When I have to die, I would like to die
on a day of rain—
long rain, slow rain, the kind you think will never end.

And I would like to have whatever little ceremony there might be
take place while the rain is shoveled and shoveled out of the sky,

and anyone who comes must travel, slowly and with thought,
as around the edges of the great swamp.

Field Near Linden, Alabama

For hours
they float in the distance—
finally they drift down
like black shingles
from some old temple of the sun,
so I know, somewhere in the world
the terrible cleansing
has begun.
Once, across a field,
a dozen of them sat in a tree.
I stopped the car and walked toward them
until they were above me,
huge and shifty,
in their leather wings,
and what was below them, in the grass,
was clearly dead.
The story about Jesus in the cave
is a good one,
but when is it ever like that,
as sharp as lightning
or even the way the green sea does everything—
quickly,
and with such grace?
Clumsy and slow,
the birds clattered down, and huddled—
their beaks were soft as spoons,
but they bent to their labor
with a will, until
their bellies swelled,

they could hardly climb back into the air
and go flapping away.
A year later
I cross the field again, and in that hot place
the grass rises thick and clean, it
shines like the sea.

Gannets

I am watching the white gannets
blaze down into the water
with the power of blunt spears
and a stunning accuracy—
even though the sea is riled and boiling
and gray with fog
and the fish
are nowhere to be seen,
they fall, they explode into the water
like white gloves,
then they vanish,
then they climb out again,
from the cliff of the wave,
like white flowers—
and still I think
that nothing in this world moves
but as a positive power—
even the fish, finning down into the current
or collapsing
in the red purse of the beak,
are only interrupted from their own pursuit
of whatever it is
that fills their bellies—
and I say:
life is real,
and pain is real,
but death is an imposter,
and if I could be what once I was,
like the wolf or the bear
standing on the cold shore,
I would still see it—

how the fish simply escape, this time,
or how they slide down into a black fire
for a moment,
then rise from the water inseparable
from the gannets' wings.

Whelks

Here are the perfect
fans of the scallops,
quahogs, and weedy mussels
still holding their orange fruit—
and here are the whelks—
whirlwinds,
each the size of a fist,
but always cracked and broken—
clearly they have been traveling
under the sky-blue waves
for a long time.
All my life
I have been restless—
I have felt there is something
more wonderful than gloss—
than wholeness—
than staying at home.
I have not been sure what it is.
But every morning on the wide shore
I pass what is perfect and shining
to look for the whelks, whose edges
have rubbed so long against the world
they have snapped and crumbled—
they have almost vanished,
with the last relinquishing
of their unrepeatable energy,
back into everything else.
When I find one
I hold it in my hand,
I look out over that shaking fire,
I shut my eyes. Not often,

but now and again there's a moment
when the heart cries aloud:
yes, I am willing to be
that wild darkness,
that long, blue body of light.

Alligator Poem

I knelt down
at the edge of the water,
and if the white birds standing
in the tops of the trees whistled any warning
I didn't understand,
I drank up to the very moment it came
crashing toward me,
its tail flailing
like a bundle of swords,
slashing the grass,
and the inside of its cradle-shaped mouth
gaping,
and rimmed with teeth—
and that's how I almost died
of foolishness
in beautiful Florida.
But I didn't.
I leaped aside, and fell,
and it streamed past me, crushing everything in its path
as it swept down to the water
and threw itself in,
and, in the end,
this isn't a poem about foolishness
but about how I rose from the ground
and saw the world as if for the second time,
the way it really is.
The water, that circle of shattered glass,
healed itself with a slow whisper
and lay back
with the back-lit light of polished steel,

and the birds, in the endless waterfalls of the trees,
shook open the snowy pleats of their wings, and drifted away,
while, for a keepsake, and to steady myself,
I reached out,
I picked the wild flowers from the grass around me—
blue stars
and blood-red trumpets
on long green stems—
for hours in my trembling hands they glittered
like fire.

Hawk

This morning
  the hawk
    rose up
      out of the meadow's browse

and swung over the lake—
  it settled
    on the small black dome
      of a dead pine,

alert as an admiral,
  its profile
    distinguished with sideburns
      the color of smoke,

and I said: remember
  this is not something
    of the red fire, this is
      heaven's fistful

of death and destruction,
  and the hawk hooked
    one exquisite foot
      onto a last twig

to look deeper
  into the yellow reeds
    along the edges of the water
      and I said: remember

the tree, the cave,
   the white lily of resurrection,
      and that's when it simply lifted
         its golden feet and floated

into the wind, belly-first,
   and then it cruised along the lake—
      all the time its eyes fastened
         harder than love on some

unimportant rustling in the
   yellow reeds—and then it
      seemed to crouch high in the air, and then it
      turned into a white blade, which fell.

Goldfinches

In the fields
we let them have—
in the fields
we don't want yet—

where thistles rise
out of the marshlands of spring, and spring open—
each bud
a settlement of riches—

a coin of reddish fire—
the finches
wait for midsummer,
for the long days,

for the brass heat,
for the seeds to begin to form in the hardening thistles,
dazzling as the teeth of mice,
but black,

filling the face of every flower.
Then they drop from the sky.
A buttery gold,
they swing on the thistles, they gather

the silvery down, they carry it
in their finchy beaks
to the edges of the fields,
to the trees,

as though their minds were on fire
with the flower of one perfect idea—
and there they build their nests
and lay their pale-blue eggs,

every year,
and every year
the hatchlings wake in the swaying branches,
in the silver baskets,

and love the world.
Is it necessary to say any more?
Have you heard them singing in the wind, above the final fields?
Have you ever been so happy in your life?

Rice

It grew in the black mud.
It grew under the tiger's orange paws.
Its stems thinner than candles, and as straight.
Its leaves like the feathers of egrets, but green.
The grains cresting, wanting to burst.
Oh, blood of the tiger.

I don't want you just to sit down at the table.
I don't want you just to eat, and be content.
I want you to walk out into the fields
where the water is shining, and the rice has risen.
I want you to stand there, far from the white tablecloth.
I want you to fill your hands with the mud, like a blessing.

Poppies

The poppies send up their
orange flares; swaying
in the wind, their congregations
are a levitation

of bright dust, of thin
and lacy leaves.
There isn't a place
in this world that doesn't

sooner or later drown
in the indigos of darkness,
but now, for a while,
the roughage

shines like a miracle
as it floats above everything
with its yellow hair.
Of course nothing stops the cold,

black, curved blade
from hooking forward—
of course
loss is the great lesson.

But also I say this: that light
is an invitation
to happiness,
and that happiness,

when it's done right,
is a kind of holiness,
palpable and redemptive.
Inside the bright fields,

touched by their rough and spongy gold,
I am washed and washed
in the river
of earthly delight—

and what are you going to do—
what can you do
about it—
deep, blue night?

A Certain Sharpness in the Morning Air

In the morning
it shuffles, unhurried,
across the wet fields
in its black slippers,
in its coal-colored coat
with the white stripe like a river
running down its spine—
a glossy animal with a quick temper
and two bulbs of such diatribe under its tail
that when I see it I pray
not to be noticed—
not to be struck
by the flat boards of its anger—
for the whole haul of its smell
is unendurable—
like tragedy
that can't be borne,
like death
that has to be buried, or burned—
but a little of it is another story—
for it's true, isn't it,
in our world,
that the petals pooled with nectar, and the polished thorns
are a single thing—
that even the purest light, lacking the robe of darkness,
would be without expression—
that love itself, without its pain, would be
no more than a shruggable comfort.
Lately, I have noticed, when the skunk's temper has tilted
in the distance,

and the acids are floating everywhere,
and I am touched, it is all, even in my nostrils and my throat,
   as the brushing of thorns;
and I stand there
thinking of the old, wild life of the fields, when, as I remember it,
I was shaggy, and beautiful,
like the rose.

A Bitterness

I believe you did not have a happy life.
I believe you were cheated.
I believe your best friends were loneliness and misery.
I believe your busiest enemies were anger and depression.
I believe joy was a game you could never play without stumbling.
I believe comfort, though you craved it, was forever a stranger.
I believe music had to be melancholy or not at all.
I believe no trinket, no precious metal, shone so bright as
    your bitterness.
I believe you lay down at last in your coffin none the wiser and
    unassuaged.
Oh, cold and dreamless under the wild, amoral, reckless, peaceful
    flowers of the hillsides.

Morning

Salt shining behind its glass cylinder.
Milk in a blue bowl. The yellow linoleum.
The cat stretching her black body from the pillow.
The way she makes her curvaceous response to the small, kind gesture.
Then laps the bowl clean.
Then wants to go out into the world
where she leaps lightly and for no apparent reason across the lawn,
then sits, perfectly still, in the grass.
I watch her a little while, thinking:
what more could I do with wild words?
I stand in the cold kitchen, bowing down to her.
I stand in the cold kitchen, everything wonderful around me.

Water Snake

I saw him
in a dry place
on a hot day,
a traveler
making his way
from one pond
to another,
and he lifted up
his chary face
and looked at me
with his gravel eyes,
and the feather of his tongue
shot in and out
of his otherwise clamped mouth,
and I stopped on the path
to give him room,
and he went past me
with his head high,
loathing me, I think,
for my long legs,
my poor body, like a post,
my many fingers,
for he didn't linger
but, touching the other side of the path,
he headed, in long lunges and quick heaves,
straight to the nearest basin
of sweet black water and weeds,
and solitude—

like an old sword
that suddenly picked itself up and went off,
swinging, swinging
through the green leaves.

The Egret

Every time
but one
the little fish
and the green
and spotted frogs
know
the egret's bamboo legs
from the thin
and polished reeds
at the edge
of the silky world
of water.
Then,
in their last inch of time,
they see,
for an instant,
the white froth
of her shoulders,
and the white scrolls
of her belly,
and the white flame
of her head.
What more can you say
about such wild swimmers?
They were here,
they were silent,
they are gone, having tasted
sheer terror.
Therefore I have invented words
with which to stand back
on the weedy shore—
with which to say:
Look! Look!
What is this dark death
that opens
like a white door?

The Snowshoe Hare

The fox
is so quiet—
he moves like a red rain—
even when his
shoulders tense and then
snuggle down for an instant
against the ground
and the perfect
gate of his teeth
slams shut
there is nothing
you can hear
but the cold creek moving
over the dark pebbles
and across the field
and into the rest of the world—
and even when you find
in the morning
the feathery
scuffs of fur
of the vanished
snowshoe hare
tangled
on the pale spires
of the broken flowers
of the lost summer—
fluttering a little
but only
like the lapping threads
of the wind itself—
there is still

nothing that you can hear
but the cold creek moving
over the old pebbles
and across the field and into
another year.

The Sun

Have you ever seen
anything
in your life
more wonderful

than the way the sun,
every evening,
relaxed and easy,
floats toward the horizon

and into the clouds or the hills,
or the rumpled sea,
and is gone—
and how it slides again

out of the blackness,
every morning,
on the other side of the world,
like a red flower

streaming upward on its heavenly oils,
say, on a morning in early summer,
at its perfect imperial distance—
and have you ever felt for anything

such wild love—
do you think there is anywhere, in any language,
a word billowing enough
for the pleasure

that fills you,
as the sun
reaches out,
as it warms you

as you stand there,
empty-handed—
or have you too
turned from this world—

or have you too
gone crazy
for power,
for things?

Winter

And the waves
gush pearls
from their snowy throats
as they come
leaping
over the moss-green,
black-green,
glass-green roughage—
as they crumble
on the incline
scattering
whatever they carry
in their invisible
and motherly
hands:
stones,
seaweed,
mussels
icy and plump
with waled shells,
waiting
for the gatherers
who come flying
on their long white wings—
who comes walking,
who comes muttering:
thank you,
old dainties,

dark wreckage,
coins of the sea
in my pockets
and plenty for the gulls
and the wind still pounding
and the sea still streaming in like a mother wild with gifts—
in this world I am as rich
as I need to be.

Lonely, White Fields

Every night
the owl
with his wild monkey-face
calls through the black branches,
and the mice freeze
and the rabbits shiver
in the snowy fields—
and then there is the long, deep trough of silence
when he stops singing, and steps
into the air.
I don't know
what death's ultimate
purpose is, but I think
this: whoever dreams of holding his
life in his fist
year after year into the hundreds of years
has never considered the owl—
how he comes, exhausted,
through the snow,
through the icy trees,
past snags and vines, wheeling
out of barns and church steeples,
turning this way and that way
through the mesh of every obstacle—
undeterred by anything—
filling himself time and time again
with a red and digestible joy
sickled up from the lonely, white fields—
and how at daybreak,
as though everything had been done
that must be done, the fields

swell with a rosy light,
the owl fades
back into the branches,
the snow goes on falling
flake after perfect flake.

Hummingbird Pauses at the Trumpet Vine

Who doesn't love
roses, and who
doesn't love the lilies
of the black ponds

floating like flocks
of tiny swans,
and of course the flaming
trumpet vine

where the hummingbird comes
like a small green angel, to soak
his dark tongue
in happiness—

and who doesn't want
to live with the brisk
motor of his heart
singing

like a Schubert,
and his eyes
working and working like those days of rapture,
by van Gogh, in Arles?

Look! for most of the world
is waiting
or remembering—
most of the world is time

when we're not here,
not born yet, or died—
a slow fire
under the earth with all

our dumb wild blind cousins
who also
can't even remember anymore
their own happiness—

Look! and then we will be
like the pale cool
stones, that last almost
forever.

White Flowers

Last night
in the fields
I lay down in the darkness
to think about death,
but instead I fell asleep,
as if in a vast and sloping room
filled with those white flowers
that open all summer,
sticky and untidy,
in the warm fields.
When I woke
the morning light was just slipping
in front of the stars,
and I was covered
with blossoms.
I don't know
how it happened—
I don't know
if my body went diving down
under the sugary vines
in some sleep-sharpened affinity
with the depths, or whether
that green energy
rose like a wave
and curled over me, claiming me
in its husky arms.
I pushed them away, but I didn't rise.
Never in my life had I felt so plush,
or so slippery,
or so resplendently empty.

Never in my life
had I felt myself so near
that porous line
where my own body was done with
and the roots and the stems and the flowers
began.

October

1

There's this shape, black as the entrance to a cave.
A longing wells up in its throat
like a blossom
as it breathes slowly.

What does the world
mean to you if you can't trust it
to go on shining when you're

not there? And there's
a tree, long-fallen; once
the bees flew to it, like a procession
of messengers, and filled it
with honey.

2

I said to the chickadee, singing his heart out in the
    green pine tree:

little dazzler,
little song,
little mouthful.

3

The shape climbs up out of the curled grass. It
grunts into view. There is no measure
for the confidence at the bottom of its eyes—
there is no telling
the suppleness of its shoulders as it turns
and yawns.

                 Near the fallen tree
something—a leaf snapped loose
from the branch and fluttering down—tries to pull me
into its trap of attention.

4

It pulls me
into its trap of attention.

And when I turn again, the bear is gone.

5

Look, hasn't my body already felt
like the body of a flower?

6

Look, I want to love this world
as though it's the last chance I'm ever going to get
to be alive
and know it.

7

Sometimes in late summer I won't touch anything, not
the flowers, not the blackberries
brimming in the thickets; I won't drink
from the pond; I won't name the birds or the trees;
I won't whisper my own name.

One morning
the fox came down the hill, glittering and confident,
and didn't see me—and I thought:

so this is the world.
I'm not in it.
It is beautiful.

FROM

House of Light

———— ❧ ————

(1 9 9 0)

Some Questions You Might Ask

Is the soul solid, like iron?
Or is it tender and breakable, like
the wings of a moth in the beak of the owl?
Who has it, and who doesn't?
I keep looking around me.
The face of the moose is as sad
as the face of Jesus.
The swan opens her white wings slowly.
In the fall, the black bear carries leaves into the darkness.
One question leads to another.
Does it have a shape? Like an iceberg?
Like the eye of a hummingbird?
Does it have one lung, like the snake and the scallop?
Why should I have it, and not the anteater
who loves her children?
Why should I have it, and not the camel?
Come to think of it, what about the maple trees?
What about the blue iris?
What about all the little stones, sitting alone in the moonlight?
What about roses, and lemons, and their shining leaves?
What about the grass?

Moccasin Flowers

All my life,
   so far,
      I have loved
         more than one thing,

including the mossy hooves
   of dreams, including
      the spongy litter
         under the tall trees.

In spring
   the moccasin flowers
      reach for the crackling
         lick of the sun

and burn down. Sometimes,
   in the shadows,
      I see the hazy eyes,
         the lamb-lips

of oblivion,
   its deep drowse,
      and I can imagine a new nothing
         in the universe,

the matted leaves splitting
   open, revealing
      the black planks
         of the stairs.

But all my life—so far—
  I have loved best
    how the flowers rise
      and open, how

the pink lungs of their bodies
  enter the fire of the world
    and stand there shining
      and willing—the one

thing they can do before
  they shuffle forward
    into the floor of darkness, they
      become the trees.

The Buddha's Last Instruction

"Make of yourself a light,"
said the Buddha,
before he died.
I think of this every morning
as the east begins
to tear off its many clouds
of darkness, to send up the first
signal—a white fan
streaked with pink and violet,
even green.
An old man, he lay down
between two sala trees,
and he might have said anything,
knowing it was his final hour.
The light burns upward,
it thickens and settles over the fields.
Around him, the villagers gathered
and stretched forward to listen.
Even before the sun itself
hangs, disattached, in the blue air,
I am touched everywhere
by its ocean of yellow waves.
No doubt he thought of everything
that had happened in his difficult life.
And then I feel the sun itself
as it blazes over the hills,
like a million flowers on fire—
clearly I'm not needed,

yet I feel myself turning
into something of inexplicable value.
Slowly, beneath the branches,
he raised his head.
He looked into the faces of that frightened crowd.

Spring

Somewhere
   a black bear
      has just risen from sleep
      and is staring

down the mountain.
   All night
      in the brisk and shallow restlessness
      of early spring

I think of her,
   her four black fists
      flicking the gravel,
        her tongue

like a red fire
   touching the grass,
      the cold water.
        There is only one question:

how to love this world.
   I think of her
      rising
        like a black and leafy ledge

to sharpen her claws against
   the silence
      of the trees.
        Whatever else

my life is
    with its poems
        and its music
            and its glass cities,

it is also this dazzling darkness
    coming
        down the mountain,
            breathing and tasting;

all day I think of her—
    her white teeth,
        her wordlessness,
            her perfect love.

Singapore

In Singapore, in the airport,
a darkness was ripped from my eyes.
In the women's restroom, one compartment stood open.
A woman knelt there, washing something
  in the white bowl.

Disgust argued in my stomach
and I felt, in my pocket, for my ticket.

A poem should always have birds in it.
Kingfishers, say, with their bold eyes and gaudy wings.
Rivers are pleasant, and of course trees.
A waterfall, or if that's not possible, a fountain
  rising and falling.
A person wants to stand in a happy place, in a poem.

When the woman turned I could not answer her face.
Her beauty and her embarrassment struggled together, and
  neither could win.
She smiled and I smiled. What kind of nonsense is this?
Everybody needs a job.

Yes, a person wants to stand in a happy place, in a poem.
But first we must watch her as she stares down at her labor,
  which is dull enough.
She is washing the tops of the airport ashtrays, as big as
  hubcaps, with a blue rag.
Her small hands turn the metal, scrubbing and rinsing.
She does not work slowly, nor quickly, but like a river.
Her dark hair is like the wing of a bird.

I don't doubt for a moment that she loves her life.
And I want her to rise up from the crust and the slop
   and fly down to the river.
This probably won't happen.
But maybe it will.
If the world were only pain and logic, who would want it?

Of course, it isn't.
Neither do I mean anything miraculous, but only
the light that can shine out of a life. I mean
the way she unfolded and refolded the blue cloth,
the way her smile was only for my sake; I mean
the way this poem is filled with trees, and birds.

The Hermit Crab

Once I looked inside
   the darkness
      of a shell folded like a pastry,
         and there was a fancy face—

or almost a face—
   it turned away
      and frisked up its brawny forearms
         so quickly

against the light
   and my looking in
      I scarcely had time to see it,
         gleaming

under the pure white roof
   of old calcium.
      When I set it down, it hurried
         along the tideline

of the sea,
   which was slashing along as usual,
      shouting and hissing
         toward the future,

turning its back
   with every tide on the past,
      leaving the shore littered
         every morning

with more ornaments of death—
   what a pearly rubble
      from which to choose a house
      like a white flower—

and what a rebellion
   to leap into it
   and hold on,
         connecting everything,

the past to the future—
   which is of course the miracle—
      which is the only argument there is
      against the sea.

Lilies

I have been thinking
about living
like the lilies
that blow in the fields.

They rise and fall
in the wedge of the wind,
and have no shelter
from the tongues of the cattle,

and have no closets or cupboards,
and have no legs.
Still I would like to be
as wonderful

as that old idea.
But if I were a lily
I think I would wait all day
for the green face

of the hummingbird
to touch me.
What I mean is,
could I forget myself

even in those feathery fields?
When van Gogh
preached to the poor
of course he wanted to save someone—

most of all himself.
He wasn't a lily,
and wandering through the bright fields
only gave him more ideas

it would take his life to solve.
I think I will always be lonely
in this world, where the cattle
graze like a black and white river—

where the ravishing lilies
melt, without protest, on their tongues—
where the hummingbird, whenever there is a fuss,
just rises and floats away.

The Swan

Across the wide waters
    something comes
        floating—a slim
        and delicate

ship, filled
    with white flowers—
        and it moves
        on its miraculous muscles

as though time didn't exist,
    as though bringing such gifts
        to the dry shore
        was a happiness

almost beyond bearing.
    And now it turns its dark eyes,
        it rearranges
        the clouds of its wings,

it trails
    an elaborate webbed foot,
        the color of charcoal.
        Soon it will be here.

Oh, what shall I do
    when that poppy-colored beak
        rests in my hand?
        Said Mrs. Blake of the poet:

I miss my husband's company—
    he is so often
        in paradise.
            Of course! the path to heaven

doesn't lie down in flat miles.
    It's in the imagination
        with which you perceive
            this world,

and the gestures
    with which you honor it.
        Oh, what will I do, what will I say, when those
            white wings
            touch the shore?

Indonesia

On the curving, dusty roads
we drove through the plantations
where the pickers balanced on the hot hillsides—
then we climbed toward the green trees,
toward the white scarves of the clouds,
to the inn that is never closed
in this island of fairest weather.
The sun hung like a stone,
time dripped away like a steaming river
and from somewhere a dry tongue lashed out
its single motto: now and forever.
And the pickers balanced on the hot hillsides
like gray and blue blossoms,
wrapped in their heavy layers of clothes
against the whips of the branches
in that world of leaves no poor man,
with a brown face and an empty sack,
has ever picked his way out of.
At the inn we stepped from the car
to the garden, where tea
was brought to us scalding in white cups from the fire.
Don't ask if it was the fire of honey
or the fire of death, don't ask
if we were determined to live, at last,
with merciful hearts. We sat
among the unforgettable flowers.
We let the white cups cool before
we raised them to our lips.

Some Herons

A blue preacher
flew toward the swamp,
in slow motion.

On the leafy banks,
an old Chinese poet,
hunched in the white gown of his wings,

was waiting.
The water
was the kind of dark silk

that has silver lines
shot through it
when it is touched by the wind

or is splashed upward,
in a small, quick flower,
by the life beneath it.

The preacher
made his difficult landing,
his skirts up around his knees.

The poet's eyes
flared, just as a poet's eyes
are said to do

when the poet is awakened
from the forest of meditation.
It was summer.

It was only a few moments past the sun's rising,
which meant that the whole long sweet day
lay before them.

They greeted each other,
rumpling their gowns for an instant,
and then smoothing them.

They entered the water,
and instantly two more herons—
equally as beautiful—

joined them and stood just beneath them
in the black, polished water
where they fished, all day.

Five A.M. in the Pinewoods

I'd seen
their hoofprints in the deep
needles and knew
they ended the long night

under the pines, walking
like two mute
and beautiful women toward
the deeper woods, so I

got up in the dark and
went there. They came
slowly down the hill
and looked at me sitting under

the blue trees, shyly
they stepped
closer and stared
from under their thick lashes and even

nibbled some damp
tassels of weeds. This
is not a poem about a dream,
though it could be.

This is a poem about the world
that is ours, or could be.
Finally
one of them—I swear it!—

would have come to my arms.
But the other
stamped sharp hoof in the
pine needles like

the tap of sanity,
and they went off together through
the trees. When I woke
I was alone,

I was thinking:
so this is how you swim inward,
so this is how you flow outward,
so this is how you pray.

Little Owl Who Lives in the Orchard

His beak could open a bottle,
and his eyes—when he lifts their soft lids—
go on reading something
just beyond your shoulder—
Blake, maybe,
or the Book of Revelation.

Never mind that he eats only
the black-smocked crickets,
and dragonflies if they happen
to be out late over the ponds, and of course
the occasional festal mouse.
Never mind that he is only a memo
from the offices of fear—

it's not size but surge that tells us
when we're in touch with something real,
and when I hear him in the orchard
fluttering
down the little aluminum
ladder of his scream—
when I see his wings open, like two black ferns,

a flurry of palpitations
as cold as sleet
rackets across the marshlands
of my heart,
like a wild spring day.

Somewhere in the universe,
in the gallery of important things,
the babyish owl, ruffled and rakish,
sits on its pedestal.
Dear, dark dapple of plush!
A message, reads the label,
from that mysterious conglomerate:
Oblivion and Co.
The hooked head stares
from its blouse of dark, feathery lace.
It could be a valentine.

The Kookaburras

In every heart there is a coward and a procrastinator.
In every heart there is a god of flowers, just waiting
to come out of its cloud and lift its wings.
The kookaburras, kingfishers, pressed against the edge of
their cage, they asked me to open the door.
Years later I wake in the night and remember how I said to them,
no, and walked away.
They had the brown eyes of soft-hearted dogs.
They didn't want to do anything so extraordinary, only to fly
home to their river.
By now I suppose the great darkness has covered them.
As for myself, I am not yet a god of even the palest flowers.
Nothing else has changed either.
Someone tosses their white bones to the dung-heap.
The sun shines on the latch of their cage.
I lie in the dark, my heart pounding.

The Lilies Break Open Over the Dark Water

Inside
    that mud-hive, that gas-sponge,
        that reeking
            leaf-yard, that rippling

dream-bowl, the leeches'
    flecked and swirling
        broth of life, as rich
            as Babylon,

the fists crack
    open and the wands
        of the lilies
            quicken, they rise

like pale poles
    with their wrapped beaks of lace;
        one day
            they tear the surface,

the next they break open
    over the dark water.
        And there you are
            on the shore,

fitful and thoughtful, trying
    to attach them to an idea—
        some news of your own life.
            But the lilies

are slippery and wild—they are
      devoid of meaning, they are
         simply doing,
               from the deepest

spurs of their being,
      what they are impelled to do
         every summer.
               And so, dear sorrow, are you.

Nature

All night
   in and out the slippery shadows
     the owl hunted,
       the beads of blood

scarcely dry on the hooked beak before
   hunger again seized him
     and he fell, snipping
       the life from some plush breather,

and floated away
   into the crooked branches
     of the trees, that all night
       went on lapping

the sunken rain, and growing,
   bristling life
     spreading through all their branches
       as one by one

they tossed the white moon upward
   on its slow way
     to another morning
       in which nothing new

would ever happen,
   which is the true gift of nature,
     which is the reason
       we love it.

Forgive me.
   For hours I had tried to sleep
     and failed;
       restless and wild,

I could settle on nothing
   and fell, in envy
     of the things of darkness
       following their sleepy course—

the root and branch, the bloodied beak—
   even the screams from the cold leaves
     were as red songs that rose and fell
      in their accustomed place.

The Ponds

Every year
the lilies
are so perfect
I can hardly believe

their lapped light crowding
the black,
mid-summer ponds.
Nobody could count all of them—

the muskrats swimming
among the pads and the grasses
can reach out
their muscular arms and touch

only so many, they are that
rife and wild.
But what in this world
is perfect?

I bend closer and see
how this one is clearly lopsided—
and that one wears an orange blight—
and this one is a glossy cheek

half nibbled away—
and that one is a slumped purse
full of its own
unstoppable decay.

Still, what I want in my life
is to be willing
to be dazzled—
to cast aside the weight of facts

and maybe even
to float a little
above this difficult world.
I want to believe I am looking

into the white fire of a great mystery.
I want to believe that the imperfections are nothing—
that the light is everything—that it is more than the sum
of each flawed blossom rising and fading. And I do.

The Summer Day

Who made the world?
Who made the swan, and the black bear?
Who made the grasshopper?
This grasshopper, I mean—
the one who has flung herself out of the grass,
the one who is eating sugar out of my hand,
who is moving her jaws back and forth instead of up and down—
who is gazing around with her enormous and complicated eyes.
Now she lifts her pale forearms and thoroughly washes her face.
Now she snaps her wings open, and floats away.
I don't know exactly what a prayer is.
I do know how to pay attention, how to fall down
into the grass, how to kneel down in the grass,
how to be idle and blessed, how to stroll through the fields,
which is what I have been doing all day.
Tell me, what else should I have done?
Doesn't everything die at last, and too soon?
Tell me, what is it you plan to do
with your one wild and precious life?

Roses, Late Summer

What happens
to the leaves after
they turn red and golden and fall
away? What happens

to the singing birds
when they can't sing
any longer? What happens
to their quick wings?

Do you think there is any
personal heaven
for any of us?
Do you think anyone,

the other side of that darkness,
will call to us, meaning us?
Beyond the trees
the foxes keep teaching their children

to live in the valley.
So they never seem to vanish, they are always there
in the blossom of light
that stands up every morning

in the dark sky.
And over one more set of hills,
along the sea,
the last roses have opened their factories of sweetness

and are giving it back to the world.
If I had another life
I would want to spend it all on some
unstinting happiness.

I would be a fox, or a tree
full of waving branches.
I wouldn't mind being a rose
in a field full of roses.

Fear has not yet occurred to them, nor ambition.
Reason they have not yet thought of.
Neither do they ask how long they must be roses, and then what.
Or any other foolish question.

Maybe

Sweet Jesus, talking
   his melancholy madness,
      stood up in the boat
         and the sea lay down,

silky and sorry.
   So everybody was saved
      that night.
         But you know how it is

when something
   different crosses
      the threshold—the uncles
         mutter together,

the women walk away,
   the young brother begins
      to sharpen his knife.
         Nobody knows what the soul is.

It comes and goes
   like the wind over the water—
      sometimes, for days,
         you don't think of it.

Maybe, after the sermon,
   after the multitude was fed,
      one or two of them felt
         the soul slip forth

like a tremor of pure sunlight,
   before exhaustion,
      that wants to swallow everything,
        gripped their bones and left them

miserable and sleepy,
   as they are now, forgetting
      how the wind tore at the sails
        before he rose and talked to it—

tender and luminous and demanding
   as he always was—
      a thousand times more frightening
        than the killer sea.

White Owl Flies Into and Out of the Field

Coming down
out of the freezing sky
with its depths of light,
like an angel,
or a buddha with wings,
it was beautiful
and accurate,
striking the snow and whatever was there
with a force that left the imprint
of the tips of its wings—
five feet apart—and the grabbing
thrust of its feet,
and the indentation of what had been running
through the white valleys
of the snow—

and then it rose, gracefully,
and flew back to the frozen marshes,
to lurk there,
like a little lighthouse,
in the blue shadows—
so I thought:
maybe death
isn't darkness, after all,
but so much light
wrapping itself around us—

as soft as feathers—
that we are instantly weary
of looking, and looking, and shut our eyes,
not without amazement,
and let ourselves be carried,
as through the translucence of mica,
to the river
that is without the least dapple or shadow—
that is nothing but light—scalding, aortal light—
in which we are washed and washed
out of our bones.

FROM

Dream Work

❦

(1 9 8 6)

Dogfish

Some kind of relaxed and beautiful thing
kept flickering in with the tide
and looking around.
Black as a fisherman's boot,
with a white belly.

If you asked for a picture I would have to draw a smile
under the perfectly round eyes and above the chin,
which was rough
as a thousand sharpened nails.

And you know
what a smile means,
don't you?

❧

I wanted
the past to go away, I wanted
to leave it, like another country; I wanted
my life to close, and open
like a hinge, like a wing, like the part of the song
    where it falls
down over the rocks: an explosion, a discovery;
    I wanted
to hurry into the work of my life; I wanted to know,
whoever I was, I was

alive
for a little while.

It was evening, and no longer summer.
Three small fish, I don't know what they were,
huddled in the highest ripples
as it came swimming in again, effortless, the whole body
one gesture, one black sleeve
that could fit easily around
the bodies of three small fish.

Also I wanted
to be able to love. And we all know
how that one goes,
don't we?

Slowly

the dogfish tore open the soft basins of water.

You don't want to hear the story
of my life, and anyway
I don't want to tell it, I want to listen

to the enormous waterfalls of the sun.

And anyway it's the same old story—
a few people just trying,
one way or another,
to survive.

Mostly, I want to be kind.
And nobody, of course, is kind,
or mean,
for a simple reason.

And nobody gets out of it, having to
swim through the fires to stay in
this world.

And look! look! look! I think those little fish
better wake up and dash themselves away
from the hopeless future that is
bulging toward them.

And probably,
if they don't waste time
looking for an easier world,

they can do it.

Morning Poem

Every morning
the world
is created.
Under the orange

sticks of the sun
the heaped
ashes of the night
turn into leaves again

and fasten themselves to the high branches—
and the ponds appear
like black cloth
on which are painted islands

of summer lilies.
If it is your nature
to be happy
you will swim away along the soft trails

for hours, your imagination
alighting everywhere.
And if your spirit
carries within it

the thorn
that is heavier than lead—
if it's all you can do
to keep on trudging—

there is still
somewhere deep within you
a beast shouting that the earth
is exactly what it wanted—

each pond with its blazing lilies
is a prayer heard and answered
lavishly,
every morning,

whether or not
you have ever dared to be happy,
whether or not
you have ever dared to pray.

Rage

You are the dark song
of the morning;
serious and slow,
you shave, you dress,
you descend the stairs
in your public clothes
and drive away, you become
the wise and powerful one
who makes all the days
possible in the world.
But you were also the red song
in the night,
stumbling through the house
to the child's bed,
to the damp rose of her body,
leaving your bitter taste.
And forever those nights snarl
the delicate machinery of the days.
When the child's mother smiles
you see on her cheekbones
a truth you will never confess;
and you see how the child grows—
timidly, crouching in corners.
Sometimes in the wide night
you hear the most mournful cry,
a ravished and terrible moment.
In your dreams she's a tree
that will never come to leaf—
in your dreams she's a watch
you dropped on the dark stones

till no one could gather the fragments—
in your dreams you have sullied and murdered,
and dreams do not lie.

Wild Geese

You do not have to be good.
You do not have to walk on your knees
for a hundred miles through the desert, repenting.
You only have to let the soft animal of your body
      love what it loves.
Tell me about despair, yours, and I will tell you mine.
Meanwhile the world goes on.
Meanwhile the sun and the clear pebbles of the rain
are moving across the landscapes,
over the prairies and the deep trees,
the mountains and the rivers.
Meanwhile the wild geese, high in the clean blue air,
are heading home again.
Whoever you are, no matter how lonely,
the world offers itself to your imagination,
calls to you like the wild geese, harsh and exciting—
over and over announcing your place
in the family of things.

Robert Schumann

Hardly a day passes I don't think of him
in the asylum: younger

than I am now, trudging the long road down
through madness toward death.

Everywhere in this world his music
explodes out of itself, as he

could not. And now I understand
something so frightening, and wonderful—

how the mind clings to the road it knows, rushing
through crossroads, sticking

like lint to the familiar. So!
Hardly a day passes I don't

think of him: nineteen, say, and it is
spring in Germany

and he has just met a girl named Clara.
He turns the corner,

he scrapes the dirt from his soles,
he runs up the dark staircase, humming.

Starfish

In the sea rocks,
   in the stone pockets
      under the tide's lip,
         in water dense as blindness

they slid
   like sponges,
      like too many thumbs.
         I knew this, and what I wanted

was to draw my hands back
   from the water—what I wanted
      was to be willing
         to be afraid.

But I stayed there,
   I crouched on the stone wall
      while the sea poured its harsh song
         through the sluices,

while I waited for the gritty lightning
   of their touch, while I stared
      down through the tide's leaving
         where sometimes I could see them—

their stubborn flesh
   lounging on my knuckles.
      What good does it do
         to lie all day in the sun

loving what is easy?
  It never grew easy,
    but at last I grew peaceful:
      all summer

my fear diminished
  as they bloomed through the water
    like flowers, like flecks
      of an uncertain dream,

while I lay on the rocks, reaching
  into the darkness, learning
    little by little to love
      our only world.

The Journey

One day you finally knew
what you had to do, and began,
though the voices around you
kept shouting
their bad advice—
though the whole house
began to tremble
and you felt the old tug
at your ankles.
"Mend my life!"
each voice cried.
But you didn't stop.
You knew what you had to do,
though the wind pried
with its stiff fingers
at the very foundations,
though their melancholy
was terrible.
It was already late
enough, and a wild night,
and the road full of fallen
branches and stones.
But little by little,
as you left their voices behind,
the stars began to burn
through the sheets of clouds,
and there was a new voice
which you slowly
recognized as your own,
that kept you company
as you strode deeper and deeper

into the world,
determined to do
the only thing you could do—
determined to save
the only life you could save.

A Visitor

My father, for example,
who was young once
and blue-eyed,
returns
on the darkest of nights
to the porch and knocks
wildly at the door,
and if I answer
I must be prepared
for his waxy face,
for his lower lip
swollen with bitterness.
And so, for a long time,
I did not answer,
but slept fitfully
between his hours of rapping.
But finally there came the night
when I rose out of my sheets
and stumbled down the hall.
The door fell open

and I knew I was saved
and could bear him,
pathetic and hollow,
with even the least of his dreams
frozen inside him,
and the meanness gone.
And I greeted him and asked him
into the house,
and lit the lamp,

and looked into his blank eyes
in which at last
I saw what a child must love,
I saw what love might have done
had we loved in time.

Stanley Kunitz

I used to imagine him
coming from the house, like Merlin
strolling with important gestures
through the garden
where everything grows so thickly,
where birds sing, little snakes lie
on the boughs, thinking of nothing
but their own good lives,
where petals float upward,
their colors exploding,
and trees open their moist
pages of thunder—
it has happened every summer for years.

But now I know more
about the great wheel of growth,
and decay, and rebirth,
and know my vision for a falsehood.
Now I see him coming from the house—
I see him on his knees,
cutting away the diseased, the superfluous,
coaxing the new,
knowing that the hour of fulfillment
is buried in years of patience—
yet willing to labor like that
on the mortal wheel.

Oh, what good it does the heart
to know it isn't magic!
Like the human child I am

I rush to imitate—
I watch him as he bends
among the leaves and vines
to hook some weed or other;
even when I do not see him,
I think of him there
raking and trimming, stirring up
those sheets of fire
between the smothering weights of earth,
the wild and shapeless air.

One or Two Things

I

Don't bother me.
I've just
been born.

2

The butterfly's loping flight
carries it through the country of the leaves
delicately, and well enough to get it
where it wants to go, wherever that is, stopping
here and there to fuzzle the damp throats
of flowers and the black mud; up
and down it swings, frenzied and aimless; and sometimes

for long delicious moments it is perfectly
lazy, riding motionless in the breeze on the soft stalk
of some ordinary flower.

3

The god of dirt
came up to me many times and said
so many wise and delectable things, I lay
on the grass listening

to his dog voice,
crow voice,
frog voice; *now,*
he said, and *now,*

and never once mentioned *forever,*

4

which has nevertheless always been,
like a sharp iron hoof,
at the center of my mind.

5

One or two things are all you need
to travel over the blue pond, over the deep
roughage of the trees and through the stiff
flowers of lightning—some deep
memory of pleasure, some cutting
knowledge of pain.

6

But to lift the hoof!
For that you need
an idea.

7

For years and years I struggled
just to love my life. And then

the butterfly
rose, weightless, in the wind.
"Don't love your life
too much," it said,

and vanished
into the world.

The Turtle

breaks from the blue-black
skin of the water, dragging her shell
with its mossy scutes
across the shallows and through the rushes
and over the mudflats, to the uprise,
to the yellow sand,
to dig with her ungainly feet
a nest, and hunker there spewing
her white eggs down
into the darkness, and you think

of her patience, her fortitude,
her determination to complete
what she was born to do—
and then you realize a greater thing—
she doesn't consider
what she was born to do.
She's only filled
with an old blind wish.
It isn't even hers but came to her
in the rain or the soft wind,
which is a gate through which her life keeps walking.

She can't see
herself apart from the rest of the world
or the world from what she must do
every spring.
Crawling up the high hill,
luminous under the sand that has packed against her skin.
she doesn't dream
she knows

she is a part of the pond she lives in,
the tall trees are her children,
the birds that swim above her
are tied to her by an unbreakable string.

Sunrise

You can
die for it—
an idea,
or the world. People

have done so,
brilliantly,
letting
their small bodies be bound

to the stake,
creating
an unforgettable
fury of light. But

this morning,
climbing the familiar hills
in the familiar
fabric of dawn, I thought

of China,
and India
and Europe, and I thought
how the sun

blazes
for everyone just
so joyfully
as it rises

under the lashes
of my own eyes, and I thought
I am so many!
What is my name?

What is the name
of the deep breath I would take
over and over
for all of us? Call it

whatever you want, it is
happiness, it is another one
of the ways to enter
fire.

Two Kinds of Deliverance

I

Last night the geese came back,
slanting fast
from the blossom of the rising moon down
to the black pond. A muskrat
swimming in the twilight saw them and hurried

to the secret lodges to tell everyone
spring had come.

And so it had.
By morning when I went out
the last of the ice had disappeared, blackbirds
sang on the shores. Every year
the geese, returning,
do this, I don't
know how.

2

The curtains opened and there was
an old man in a headdress of feathers,
leather leggings and a vest made
from the skin of some animal. He danced

in a kind of surly rapture, and the trees
in the fields far away

began to mutter and suck up their long roots.
Slowly they advanced until they stood
pressed to the schoolhouse windows.

3

I don't know
lots of things but I know this: next year
when spring
flows over the starting point I'll think I'm going to
drown in the shimmering miles of it and then
one or two birds will fly me over
the threshold.
As for the pain
of others, of course it tries to be
abstract, but then

there flares up out of a vanished wilderness, like fire,
still blistering: the wrinkled face
of an old Chippewa
smiling, hating us,
dancing for his life.

Landscape

Isn't it plain the sheets of moss, except that
they have no tongues, could lecture
all day if they wanted about

spiritual patience? Isn't it clear
the black oaks along the path are standing
as though they were the most fragile of flowers?

Every morning I walk like this around
the pond, thinking: if the doors of my heart
ever close, I am as good as dead.

Every morning, so far, I'm alive. And now
the crows break off from the rest of the darkness
and burst up into the sky—as though

all night they had thought of what they would like
their lives to be, and imagined
their strong, thick wings.

Acid

In Jakarta,
among the venders
of flowers and soft drinks,
I saw a child
with a hideous mouth,
begging,
and I knew the wound was made
for a way to stay alive.
What I gave him
wouldn't keep a dog alive.
What he gave me
from the brown coin
of his sweating face
was a look of cunning.
I carry it
like a bead of acid
to remember how,
once in a while,
you can creep out of your own life
and become someone else—
an explosion
in that nest of wires
we call the imagination.
I will never see him
again, I suppose.
But what of this rag,
this shadow

flung like a boy's body
into the walls
of my mind, bleeding
their sour taste—
insult and anger,
the great movers?

The Moths

There's a kind of white moth, I don't know
what kind, that glimmers
by mid-May
in the forest, just
as the pink moccasin flowers
are rising.

If you notice anything,
it leads you to notice
more
and more.

And anyway
I was so full of energy.
I was always running around, looking
at this and that.

If I stopped
the pain
was unbearable.

If I stopped and thought, maybe
the world
can't be saved,
the pain
was unbearable.

Finally, I had noticed enough.
All around me in the forest
the white moths floated.

How long do they live, fluttering
in and out of the shadows?

You aren't much, I said
one day to my reflection
in a green pond,
and grinned.

The wings of the moths catch the sunlight
and burn
so brightly.

At night, sometimes,
they slip between the pink lobes
of the moccasin flowers and lie there until dawn,
motionless
in those dark halls of honey.

1945–1985: Poem for the Anniversary

Sometimes,
walking for hours through the woods,
I don't know what I'm looking for,
maybe for something
shy and beautiful to come
frisking out of the undergrowth.

Once a fawn did just that.
My dog didn't know
what dogs usually do.
And the fawn didn't know.

As for the doe, she was probably
down in Round Pond, swizzling up
the sweet marsh grass and dreaming
that everything was fine.

The way I'd like to go on living in this world
wouldn't hurt anything, I'd just go on
walking uphill and downhill, looking around,
and so what if half the time I don't know
what for—

so what if it doesn't come
to a hill of beans—

so what if I vote liberal,

and am Jewish,
or Lutheran—

or a game warden—

or a bingo addict—

and smoke a pipe?

In the films of Dachau and Auschwitz and Bergen-Belsen
the dead rise from the earth
and are piled in front of us, the starved
stare across forty years,
and lush, green, musical Germany
shows again its iron claw, which won't

ever be forgotten, which won't
ever be understood, but which did,
slowly, for years, scrape across Europe

while the rest of the world
did nothing.

Oh, you never saw
such a good leafy place, and
everything was fine, my dog and the fawn
did a little dance,
they didn't get serious.
Then the fawn clambered away through the leaves

and my gentle dog followed me away.

Oh, you never saw such a garden!
A hundred kinds of flowers in bloom!
A waterfall, for pleasure and nothing else!
The garden furniture is white,
tables and chairs in the cool shade.
A man sits there, the long afternoon before him.
He is finishing lunch, some kind
of fruits, chicken, and a salad.
A bottle of wine with a thin and beaded neck.

He fills a glass.
You can tell it is real crystal.
He lifts it to his mouth and drinks peacefully.

It is the face of Mengele.

Later
the doe came wandering back in the twilight.
She stepped through the leaves. She hesitated,
sniffing the air.

Then she knew everything.

The forest grew dark.

She nuzzled her child wildly.

The Sunflowers

Come with me
   into the field of sunflowers.
      Their faces are burnished disks,
      their dry spines

creak like ship masts,
   their green leaves,
      so heavy and many,
         fill all day with the sticky

sugars of the sun.
   Come with me
      to visit the sunflowers,
         they are shy

but want to be friends;
   they have wonderful stories
      of when they were young—
         the important weather,

the wandering crows.
   Don't be afraid
      to ask them questions!
      Their bright faces,

which follow the sun,
   will listen, and all
      those rows of seeds—
         each one a new life!—

hope for a deeper acquaintance;
  each of them, though it stands
    in a crowd of many,
      like a separate universe,

is lonely, the long work
  of turning their lives
    into a celebration
      is not easy. Come

and let us talk with those modest faces,
  the simple garments of leaves,
    the coarse roots in the earth
      so uprightly burning.

FROM

American Primitive

———— ❦ ————

(1 9 8 3)

August

When the blackberries hang
swollen in the woods, in the brambles
nobody owns, I spend

all day among the high
branches, reaching
my ripped arms, thinking

of nothing, cramming
the black honey of summer
into my mouth; all day my body

accepts what it is. In the dark
creeks that run by there is
this thick paw of my life darting among

the black bells, the leaves; there is
this happy tongue.

Mushrooms

Rain, and then
the cool pursed
lips of the wind
draw them
out of the ground—
red and yellow skulls
pummeling upward
through leaves,
through grasses,
through sand; astonishing
in their suddenness,
their quietude,
their wetness, they appear
on fall mornings, some
balancing in the earth
on one hoof
packed with poison,
others billowing
chunkily, and delicious—
those who know
walk out to gather, choosing
the benign from flocks
of glitterers, sorcerers,
russulas,
panther caps,
shark-white death angels
in their torn veils
looking innocent as sugar
but full of paralysis:
to eat
is to stagger down

fast as mushrooms themselves
when they are done being perfect
and overnight
slide back under the shining
fields of rain.

Lightning

The oaks shone
gaunt gold
on the lip
of the storm before
the wind rose,
the shapeless mouth
opened and began
its five-hour howl;
the lights
went out fast, branches
sidled over
the pitch of the roof, bounced
into the yard
that grew black
within minutes, except
for the lightning—the landscape
bulging forth like a quick
lesson in creation, then
thudding away. Inside,
as always,
it was hard to tell
fear from excitement:
how sensual
the lightning's
poured stroke! and still,
what a fire and a risk!
As always the body
wants to hide,
wants to flow toward it—strives
to balance while
fear shouts,

excitement shouts, back
and forth—each
bolt a burning river
tearing like escape through the dark
field of the other.

Egrets

Where the path closed
  down and over,
    through the scumbled leaves,
    fallen branches,
through the knotted catbrier,
  I kept going. Finally
  I could not
    save my arms
      from the thorns; soon
the mosquitoes
  smelled me, hot
    and wounded, and came
      wheeling and whining.
      And that's how I came
to the edge of the pond:
  black and empty
    except for a spindle
    of bleached reeds
at the far shore
  which, as I looked,
    wrinkled suddenly
      into three egrets—
a shower
  of white fire!
    Even half-asleep they had
    such faith in the world
that had made them—
  tilting through the water,
  unruffled, sure,
    by the laws

of their faith not logic,
they opened their wings
softly and stepped
over every dark thing.

First Snow

The snow
began here
this morning and all day
continued, its white
rhetoric everywhere
calling us back to *why, how,*
whence such beauty and *what*
the meaning; such
an oracular fever! flowing
past windows, an energy it seemed
would never ebb, never settle
less than lovely! and only now,
deep into night,
it has finally ended.
The silence
is immense,
and the heavens still hold
a million candles; nowhere
the familiar things:
stars, the moon,
the darkness we expect
and nightly turn from. Trees
glitter like castles
of ribbons, the broad fields
smolder with light, a passing
creekbed lies
heaped with shining hills;
and though the questions
that have assailed us all day
remain—not a single
answer has been found—

walking out now
into the silence and the light
under the trees,
and through the fields,
feels like one.

Ghosts

1

Have you noticed?

2

Where so many millions of powerful bawling beasts
lay down on the earth and died
it's hard to tell now
what's bone, and what merely
was once.

The golden eagle, for instance,
has a bit of heaviness in him;
moreover the huge barns
seem ready, sometimes, to ramble off
toward deeper grass.

3

1805
near the Bitterroot Mountains:
a man named Lewis kneels down
on the prairie watching

a sparrow's nest cleverly concealed in the wild hyssop
and lined with buffalo hair. The chicks,
not more than a day hatched, lean
quietly into the thick wool as if
content, after all,

to have left the perfect world and fallen,
helpless and blind
into the flowered fields and the perils
of this one.

4

In the book of the earth it is written:
nothing can die.

In the book of the Sioux it is written:
they have gone away into the earth to hide.
Nothing will coax them out again
but the people dancing.

5

Said the old-timers:
the tongue
is the sweetest meat.

Passengers shooting from train windows
could hardly miss, they were
that many.

Afterward the carcasses
stank unbelievably, and sang with flies, ribboned
with slopes of white fat,
black ropes of blood—hellhunks
in the prairie heat.

6

Have you noticed? how the rain
falls soft as the fall
of moccasins. *Have you noticed?*
how the immense circles still,
stubbornly, after a hundred years,
mark the grass where the rich droppings
from the roaring bulls
fell to the earth as the herd stood
day after day, moon after moon
in their tribal circle, outwaiting
the packs of yellow-eyed wolves that are also
have you noticed? gone now.

7

Once only, and then in a dream,
I watched while, secretly
and with the tenderness of any caring woman,
a cow gave birth
to a red calf, tongued him dry and nursed him
in a warm corner
of the clear night
in the fragrant grass
in the wild domains
of the prairie spring, and I asked them,
in my dream I knelt down and asked them
to make room for me.

Vultures

Like large dark
lazy
butterflies they sweep over
the glades looking
for death,
to eat it,
to make it vanish,
to make of it the miracle:
resurrection. No one
knows how many
they are who daily
minister so to the grassy
miles, no one
counts how many bodies
they discover
and descend to, demonstrating
each time the earth's
appetite, the unending
waterfalls of change.
No one,
moreover,
wants to ponder it,
how it will be
to feel the blood cool,
shapeliness dissolve.
Locked into
the blaze of our own bodies
we watch them
wheeling and drifting, we
honor them and we
loathe them,

however wise the doctrine,
however magnificent the cycles,
however ultimately sweet
the huddle of death to fuel
those powerful wings.

Rain in Ohio

The robin cries: *rain!*
The crow calls: *plunder!*

The blacksnake climbing
in the vines halts
his long ladder of muscle

while the thunderheads whirl up
out of the white west,

their dark hooves nicking
the tall trees as they come.

Rain, rain, rain! sings the robin
frantically, then flies for cover.

The crow hunches.
The blacksnake

pours himself swift and heavy
into the ground.

University Hospital, Boston

The trees on the hospital lawn
are lush and thriving. They too
are getting the best of care,
like you, and the anonymous many,
in the clean rooms high above this city,
where day and night the doctors keep
arriving, where intricate machines
chart with cool devotion
the murmur of the blood,
the slow patching-up of bone,
the despair of the mind.

When I come to visit and we walk out
into the light of a summer day,
we sit under the trees—
buckeyes, a sycamore and one
black walnut brooding
high over a hedge of lilacs
as old as the red-brick building
behind them, the original
hospital built before the Civil War.
We sit on the lawn together, holding hands
while you tell me: you are better.

How many young men, I wonder,
came here, wheeled on cots off the slow trains
from the red and hideous battlefields
to lie all summer in the small and stuffy chambers
while doctors did what they could, longing
for tools still unimagined, medicines still unfound,
wisdoms still unguessed at, and how many died

staring at the leaves of the trees, blind
to the terrible effort around them to keep them alive?
I look into your eyes

which are sometimes green and sometimes gray,
and sometimes full of humor, but often not,
and tell myself, you are better,
because my life without you would be
a place of parched and broken trees.
Later, walking the corridors down to the street,
I turn and step inside an empty room.
Yesterday someone was here with a gasping face.
Now the bed is made all new,
the machines have been rolled away. The silence
continues, deep and neutral,
as I stand there, loving you.

Skunk Cabbage

And now as the iron rinds over
the ponds start dissolving,
you come, dreaming of ferns and flowers
and new leaves unfolding,
upon the brash
turnip-hearted skunk cabbage
slinging its bunched leaves up
through the chilly mud.
You kneel beside it. The smell
is lurid and flows out in the most
unabashed way, attracting
into itself a continual spattering
of protein. Appalling its rough
green caves, and the thought
of the thick root nested below, stubborn
and powerful as instinct!
But these are the woods you love,
where the secret name
of every death is life again—a miracle
wrought surely not of mere turning
but of dense and scalding reenactment. Not
tenderness, not longing, but daring and brawn
pull down the frozen waterfall, the past.
Ferns, leaves, flowers, the last subtle
refinements, elegant and easeful, wait
to rise and flourish.
What blazes the trail is not necessarily pretty.

Blossom

In April
    the ponds
        open
            like black blossoms,
the moon
    swims in every one;
        there's fire
            everywhere: frogs shouting
their desire,
    their satisfaction. What
        we know: that time
            chops at us all like an iron
hoe, that death
    is a state of paralysis. What
        we long for: joy
            before death, nights
in the swale—everything else
    can wait but not
        this thrust
            from the root
of the body. What
    we know: we are more
        than blood—we are more
            than our hunger and yet
we belong
    to the moon and when the ponds
        open, when the burning
            begins the most

thoughtful among us dreams
   of hurrying down
      into the black petals,
         into the fire,
into the night where time lies shattered,
into the body of another.

White Night

All night
  I float
    in the shallow ponds
      while the moon wanders
burning,
  bone white,
    among the milky stems.
    Once
I saw her hand reach
  to touch the muskrat's
    small sleek head
      and it was lovely, oh,
I don't want to argue anymore
  about all the things
    I thought I could not
      live without! Soon
the muskrat
  will glide with another
    into their castle
      of weeds, morning
will rise from the east
  tangled and brazen,
    and before that
      difficult
and beautiful
  hurricane of light
    I want to flow out
      across the mother

of all waters,
  I want to lose myself
   on the black
    and silky currents,
yawning,
  gathering
   the tall lilies
    of sleep.

The Fish

The first fish
I ever caught
would not lie down
quiet in the pail
but flailed and sucked
at the burning
amazement of the air
and died
in the slow pouring off
of rainbows. Later
I opened his body and separated
the flesh from the bones
and ate him. Now the sea
is in me: I am the fish, the fish
glitters in me; we are
risen, tangled together, certain to fall
back to the sea. Out of pain,
and pain, and more pain
we feed this feverish plot, we are nourished
by the mystery.

Crossing the Swamp

Here is the endless
   wet thick
      cosmos, the center
         of everything—the nugget
of dense sap, branching
   vines, the dark burred
      faintly belching
         bogs. Here
is *swamp,* here
   is struggle,
      closure—
         pathless, seamless,
peerless mud. My bones
   knock together at the pale
      joints, trying
         for foothold, fingerhold,
mindhold over
   such slick crossings, deep
      hipholes, hummocks
         that sink silently
into the black, slack
   earthsoup. I feel
      not wet so much as
         painted and glittered
with the fat grassy
   mires, the rich
      and succulent marrows
         of earth—a poor

dry stick given
   one more chance by the whims
      of swamp water—a bough
         that still, after all these years,
could take root,
    sprout, branch out, bud—
       make of its life a breathing
        palace of leaves.

Humpbacks

There is, all around us,
this country
of original fire.

You know what I mean.

The sky, after all, stops at nothing, so something
        has to be holding
our bodies
in its rich and timeless stables or else
we would fly away.

Off Stellwagen
off the Cape,
the humpbacks rise. Carrying their tonnage
        of barnacles and joy
they leap through the water, they nuzzle back under it
like children
at play.

They sing, too.
And not for any reason
you can't imagine.

Three of them
rise to the surface near the bow of the boat,
then dive
deeply, their huge scarred flukes
tipped to the air.

We wait, not knowing
just where it will happen; suddenly
they smash through the surface, someone begins
shouting for joy and you realize
it is yourself as they surge
upward and you see for the first time
how huge they are, as they breach,
and dive, and breach again
through the shining blue flowers
of the split water and you see them
for some unbelievable
part of a moment against the sky—
like nothing you've ever imagined—
like the myth of the fifth morning galloping
out of darkness, pouring
heavenward, spinning; then

they crash back under those black silks
and we all fall back
together into that wet fire, you
know what I mean.

I know a captain who has seen them
playing with seaweed, swimming
through the green islands, tossing
the slippery branches into the air.

I know a whale that will come to the boat whenever
she can, and nudge it gently along the bow
with her long flipper.

I know several lives worth living.

Listen, whatever it is you try
to do with your life, nothing will ever dazzle you
like the dreams of your body,

its spirit
longing to fly while the dead-weight bones

toss their dark mane and hurry
back into the fields of glittering fire

where everything,
even the great whale,
throbs with song.

A Meeting

She steps into the dark swamp
where the long wait ends.

The secret slippery package
drops to the weeds.

She leans her long neck and tongues it
between breaths slack with exhaustion

and after a while it rises and becomes a creature
like her, but much smaller.

So now there are two. And they walk together
like a dream under the trees.

In early June, at the edge of a field
thick with pink and yellow flowers

I meet them.
I can only stare.

She is the most beautiful woman
I have ever seen.

Her child leaps among the flowers,
the blue of the sky falls over me

like silk, the flowers burn, and I want
to live my life all over again, to begin again,

to be utterly
wild.

The Sea

Stroke by
   stroke my
      body remembers that life and cries for
         the lost parts of itself—
fins, gills
   opening like flowers into
      the flesh—my legs
         want to lock and become
one muscle, I swear I know
   just what the blue-gray scales
      shingling
         the rest of me would
feel like!
   paradise! Sprawled
      in that motherlap,
         in that dreamhouse
of salt and exercise,
   what a spillage
      of nostalgia pleads
         from the very bones! how
they long to give up the long trek
   inland, the brittle
      beauty of understanding,
         and dive,
and simply
   become again a flaming body
      of blind feeling
         sleeking along

in the luminous roughage of the sea's body,
    vanished
        like victory inside that
            insucking genesis, that
roaring flamboyance, that
    perfect
        beginning and
            conclusion of our own.

Happiness

In the afternoon I watched
the she-bear; she was looking
for the secret bin of sweetness—
honey, that the bees store
in the trees' soft caves.
Black block of gloom, she climbed down
tree after tree and shuffled on
through the woods. And then
she found it! The honey-house deep
as heartwood, and dipped into it
among the swarming bees—honey and comb
she lipped and tongued and scooped out
in her black nails, until

maybe she grew full, or sleepy, or maybe
a little drunk, and sticky
down the rugs of her arms,
and began to hum and sway.
I saw her let go of the branches,
I saw her lift her honeyed muzzle
into the leaves, and her thick arms,
as though she would fly—
an enormous bee
all sweetness and wings—
down into the meadows, the perfection
of honeysuckle and roses and clover—
to float and sleep in the sheer nets
swaying from flower to flower
day after shining day.

Tecumseh

I went down not long ago
to the Mad River, under the willows
I knelt and drank from that crumpled flow, call it
what madness you will, there's a sickness
worse than the risk of death and that's
forgetting what we should never forget.
Tecumseh lived here.
The wounds of the past
are ignored, but hang on
like the litter that snags among the yellow branches,
newspapers and plastic bags, after the rains.

Where are the Shawnee now?
Do you know? Or would you have to
write to Washington, and even then,
whatever they said,
would you believe it? Sometimes

I would like to paint my body red and go out into
the glittering snow
to die.

His name meant Shooting Star.
From Mad River country north to the border
he gathered the tribes
and armed them one more time. He vowed
to keep Ohio and it took him
over twenty years to fail.

After the bloody and final fighting, at Thames,
it was over, except

his body could not be found.
It was never found,
and you can do whatever you want with that, say

his people came in the black leaves of the night
and hauled him to a secret grave, or that
he turned into a little boy again, and leaped
into a birch canoe and went
rowing home down the rivers. Anyway,
this much I'm sure of: if we ever meet him, we'll know it,
he will still be
so angry.

In Blackwater Woods

Look, the trees
are turning
their own bodies
into pillars

of light,
are giving off the rich
fragrance of cinnamon
and fulfillment,

the long tapers
of cattails
are bursting and floating away over
the blue shoulders

of the ponds,
and every pond,
no matter what its
name is, is

nameless now.
Every year
everything
I have ever learned

in my lifetime
leads back to this: the fires
and the black river of loss
whose other side

is salvation,
whose meaning
none of us will ever know.
To live in this world

you must be able
to do three things:
to love what is mortal;
to hold it

against your bones knowing
your own life depends on it;
and, when the time comes to let it go,
to let it go.

FROM

Twelve Moons

❦

(1 9 7 9)

Sleeping in the Forest

I thought the earth
remembered me, she
took me back so tenderly, arranging
her dark skirts, her pockets
full of lichens and seeds. I slept
as never before, a stone
on the riverbed, nothing
between me and the white fire of the stars
but my thoughts, and they floated
light as moths among the branches
of the perfect trees. All night
I heard the small kingdoms breathing
around me, the insects, and the birds
who do their work in the darkness. All night
I rose and fell, as if in water, grappling
with a luminous doom. By morning
I had vanished at least a dozen times
into something better.

Mussels

In the riprap,
   in the cool caves,
     in the dim and salt-refreshed
      recesses, they cling
in dark clusters,
   in barnacled fistfuls,
     in the dampness that never
      leaves, in the deeps
of high tide, in the slow
   washing away of the water
     in which they feed,
      in which the blue shells
open a little, and the orange bodies
   make a sound,
     not loud,
      not unmusical, as they take
nourishment, as the ocean
   enters their bodies. At low tide
     I am on the riprap, clattering
      with boots and a pail,
rock over rock; I choose
   the crevice, I reach
     forward into the dampness,
      my hands feeling everywhere
for the best, the biggest. Even before
   I decide which to take,
     which to twist from the wet rocks,
      which to devour,

they, who have no eyes to see with,
  see me, like a shadow,
    bending forward. Together
      they make a sound,
not loud,
  not unmusical, as they lean
    into the rocks, away
      from my grasping fingers.

The Black Snake

When the black snake
flashed onto the morning road,
and the truck could not swerve—
death, that is how it happens.

Now he lies looped and useless
as an old bicycle tire.
I stop the car
and carry him into the bushes.

He is as cool and gleaming
as a braided whip, he is as beautiful and quiet
as a dead brother.
I leave him under the leaves

and drive on, thinking
about *death:* its suddenness,
its terrible weight,
its certain coming. Yet under

reason burns a brighter fire, which the bones
have always preferred.
It is the story of endless good fortune.
It says to oblivion: not me!

It is the light at the center of every cell.
It is what sent the snake coiling and flowing forward
happily all spring through the green leaves before
he came to the road.

Spring

In April the Morgan was bred. I was chased away.
I heard the cries of the horses where I waited,
And the laughter of the men.

Later the farmer who owned the stallion
Found me and said, "She's done.
You tell your daddy he owes me fifty dollars."

I rode her home at her leisure
And let her, wherever she wanted,
Tear with her huge teeth, roughly,

Blades from the fields of spring.

Strawberry Moon

I

My great-aunt Elizabeth Fortune
stood under the honey locust trees,
the white moon over her and a young man near.
The blossoms fell down like white feathers,
the grass was warm as a bed, and the young man
full of promises, and the face of the moon
a white fire.

Later,
when the young man went away and came back with a
       bride,
Elizabeth
climbed into the attic.

2

Three women came in the night
to wash the blood away,
and burn the sheets,
and take away the child.

Was it a boy or girl?
No one remembers.

3

Elizabeth Fortune was not seen again
for forty years.

Meals were sent up,
laundry exchanged.

It was considered a solution
more proper than shame
showing itself to the village.

4

Finally, name by name, the downstairs died
or moved away,
and she had to come down,
so she did.

At sixty-one, she took in boarders,

washed their dishes,
made their beds,
spoke whatever had to be spoken,
and no more.

5

I asked my mother:
what happened to the man? She answered:

Nothing.
They had three children.
He worked in the boatyard.

I asked my mother: did they ever meet again?
No, she said,
though sometimes he would come
to the house to visit.
Elizabeth, of course, stayed upstairs.

6

Now the women are gathering
in smoke-filled rooms,
rough as politicians,
scrappy as club fighters.
And should anyone be surprised

if sometimes, when the white moon rises,
women want to lash out
with a cutting edge?

The Truro Bear

There's a bear in the Truro woods.
People have seen it—three or four,
or two, or one. I think
of the thickness of the serious woods
around the dark bowls of the Truro ponds;
I think of the blueberry fields, the blackberry tangles,
the cranberry bogs. And the sky
with its new moon, its familiar star-trails,
burns down like a brand-new heaven,
while everywhere I look on the scratchy hillsides
shadows seem to grow shoulders. Surely
a beast might be clever, be lucky, move quietly
through the woods for years, learning to stay away
from roads and houses. Common sense mutters:
it can't be true, it must be somebody's
runaway dog. But the seed
has been planted, and when has happiness ever
required much evidence to begin
its leaf-green breathing?

Entering the Kingdom

The crows see me.
They stretch their glossy necks
In the tallest branches
Of green trees. I am
Possibly dangerous, I am
Entering the kingdom.

The dream of my life
Is to lie down by a slow river
And stare at the light in the trees—
To learn something by being nothing
A little while but the rich
Lens of attention.

But the crows puff their feathers and cry
Between me and the sun,
And I should go now.
They know me for what I am.
No dreamer,
No eater of leaves.

Buck Moon—From the Field Guide to Insects

Eighty-eight thousand six-hundred
different species in North America. In the trees, the grasses
around us. Maybe more, maybe
several million on each acre of earth. This one
as well as any other. Where you are standing
at dusk. Where the moon
appears to be climbing the eastern sky. Where the wind
seems to be traveling through the trees, and the frogs
are content in their black ponds or else
why do they sing? Where you feel
a power that is not you but flows
into you like a river. Where you lie down and breathe
the sweet honey of the grass and count
the stars, where you fall asleep listening
to the simple chords repeated, repeated.
Where, resting, you feel
the perfection, the rising, the happiness
of their dark wings.

Dreams

When the rain is over
I go to the woods.
The path is a swamp, the trees still dripping.
And the creeks!
Only last week they poured smoothly,
Curled like threads about the mossy stones
And sang with the voices of birds.

Now they are swollen and driven with muds and
      ambitions.
They gallop and steam
As though, crazed by this week of rain,
They sense ahead—and desire it—
A new life in a new land
Where vines tumble thick as ship-ropes,
The ferns grow tall as trees!

They remind me of something, some other travelers—
Two great-uncles who went west years ago
And got lost in Colorado
Looking for the good life.
I have a picture of them; each is smiling,
Glad to be young and strong.
But you never know, traveling, around what bend
The dreams will curve to an end,
And what will happen then.

It was a long time ago.
Still, watching the tame creeks boil away,
My heart in sympathy pounds like a quick hoof.
I think with pride of my uncles who went west
Full of hope and vision;
I think they became healthy as animals, and rich
    as their dreams
Before they turned some corner and became
Two graves under the leaves.

The Lamps

Eight o'clock, no later,
You light the lamps,

The big one by the large window,
The small one on your desk.

They are not to see by—
It is still twilight out over the sand,

The scrub oaks and cranberries.
Even the small birds have not settled

For sleep yet, out of the reach
Of prowling foxes. No,

You light the lamps because
You are alone in your small house

And the wicks sputtering gold
Are like two visitors with good stories

They will tell slowly, in soft voices,
While the air outside turns quietly

A grainy and luminous blue.
You wish it would never change—

But of course the darkness keeps
Its appointment. Each evening,

An inscrutable presence, it has the final word
Outside every door.

Bone Poem

The litter under the tree
Where the owl eats—shrapnel

Of rat bones, gull debris—
Sinks into the wet leaves

Where time sits with her slow spoon,
Where *we* becomes singular, and a quickening

From light-years away
Saves and maintains. O holy

Protein, o hallowed lime,
O precious clay!

Tossed under the tree
The cracked bones

Of the owl's most recent feast
Lean like shipwreck, starting

The long fall back to the center—
The seepage, the flowing,

The equity: sooner or later
In the shimmering leaves

The rat will learn to fly, the owl
Will be devoured.

Aunt Leaf

Needing one, I invented her—
the great-great-aunt dark as hickory
called Shining-Leaf, or Drifting-Cloud
or The-Beauty-of-the-Night.

Dear aunt, I'd call into the leaves,
and she'd rise up, like an old log in a pool,
and whisper in a language only the two of us knew
the word that meant *follow,*

and we'd travel
cheerful as birds
out of the dusty town and into the trees
where she would change us both into something quicker—
two foxes with black feet,
two snakes green as ribbons,
two shimmering fish—
and all day we'd travel.

At day's end she'd leave me back at my own door
with the rest of my family,
who were kind, but solid as wood
and rarely wandered. While she,
old twist of feathers and birch bark,
would walk in circles wide as rain and then
float back

scattering the rags of twilight
on fluttering moth wings;

or she'd slouch from the barn like a gray opossum;

or she'd hang in the milky moonlight
burning like a medallion,

this bone dream,
this friend I had to have,
this old woman made out of leaves.

Hunter's Moon—Eating the Bear

Good friend,
it is a long afternoon.
The shadows of the pines are blue on the field.

When I find you,
I am going to turn the world inside out.
The rocks around you will melt,
your heart will fall from your body.

> *And I will step out over the fields,*

Good friend,
when I crouch beside the blades of fire,
holding a piece of your life on a knife-tip,

I will be leaning in like a spoke to the hub—
the dense orb that is all of us.

> *my body like a cupped hand*

And I will put you into my mouth, yes.
And I will swallow, yes.
So. You will come to live inside me:
muscle, layers of sweet leaves
hidden in the pink fat, the maroon flesh.

> *holding your vast power, your grace,*

Good friend,
the sun going down will signal
the end of the day, around me

      your breath, your hairiness,

the pines you can no longer see
will be twisted and small, their shadows
stretching out, still turning around

      in the small sinews of my prayers.

some invisible dead-center.

Last Days

Things are
   changing; things are starting to
     spin, snap, fly off into
       the blue sleeve of the long
         afternoon. *Oh* and *ooh*
come whistling out of the perished mouth
   of the grass, as things
turn soft, boil back
   into substance and hue. As everything,
     forgetting its own enchantment, whispers:
       I too love oblivion why not it is full
        of second chances. *Now,*
hiss the bright curls of the leaves. *Now!*
   booms the muscle of the wind.

The Black Walnut Tree

My mother and I debate:
we could sell
the black walnut tree
to the lumberman,
and pay off the mortgage.
Likely some storm anyway
will churn down its dark boughs,
smashing the house. We talk
slowly, two women trying
in a difficult time to be wise.
Roots in the cellar drains,
I say, and she replies
that the leaves are getting heavier
every year, and the fruit
harder to gather away.
But something brighter than money
moves in our blood—an edge
sharp and quick as a trowel
that wants us to dig and sow.
So we talk, but we don't do
anything. That night I dream
of my fathers out of Bohemia
filling the blue fields
of fresh and generous Ohio
with leaves and vines and orchards.
What my mother and I both know
is that we'd crawl with shame
in the emptiness we'd made
in our own and our fathers' backyard.
So the black walnut tree

swings through another year
of sun and leaping winds,
of leaves and bounding fruit,
and, month after month, the whip-
crack of the mortgage.

Wolf Moon

Now is the season
of hungry mice,
cold rabbits,
lean owls
hunkering with their lamp-eyes
in the leafless lanes
in the needled dark;
now is the season
when the kittle fox
comes to town
in the blue valley
of early morning;
now is the season
of iron rivers,
bloody crossings,
flaring winds,
birds frozen
in their tents of weeds,
their music spent
and blown like smoke
to the stone of the sky;
now is the season
of the hunter *Death;*
with his belt of knives,
his black snowshoes,
he means to cleanse
the earth of fat;
his gray shadows
are out and running—under
the moon, the pines,
down snow-filled trails they carry

the red whips of their music,
their footfalls quick as hammers,
from cabin to cabin,
from bed to bed,
from dreamer to dreamer.

The Night Traveler

Passing by, he could be anybody:
A thief, a tradesman, a doctor
On his way to a worried house.
But when he stops at your gate,
Under the room where you lie half-asleep,
You know it is not just anyone—
It is the Night Traveler.

You lean your arms on the sill
And stare down. But all you can see
Are bits of wilderness attached to him—
Twigs, loam and leaves,
Vines and blossoms. Among these
You feel his eyes, and his hands
Lifting something in the air.

He has a gift for you, but it has no name.
It is windy and wooly.
He holds it in the moonlight, and it sings
Like a newborn beast,
Like a child at Christmas,
Like your own heart as it tumbles
In love's green bed.
You take it, and he is gone.

All night—and all your life, if you are willing—
It will nuzzle your face, cold-nosed,
Like a small white wolf;
It will curl in your palm

Like a hard blue stone;
It will liquify into a cold pool
Which, when you dive into it,
Will hold you like a mossy jaw.
A bath of light. An answer.

FROM

The Night Traveler

AND

Sleeping in the Forest

(1 9 7 8)

AND FIVE POEMS

NOT PREVIOUSLY INCLUDED

IN ANY VOLUME

Aunt Elsie's Night Music

Aunt Elsie hears
Singing in the night,
So I am sent running
To search under the trees.
I stand in the dark hearing nothing—
Or, at least, not what she hears—
Uncle William singing again
Irish lullabies.
I stay awhile, then turn and go inside.
Uncle William's been dead for years.

2

Climbing the steps, I think of what to say:
"I saw a bird stretching its wings in the moonlight."
"There were marks on the grass—maybe they were
    footprints."
"Next time I'll be quicker."

3

She's as wrinkled as a leaf
You carry in your pocket for a charm
And fold and unfold.
She's so old there's no hope.
She's so crazy there's no end
To the things she thinks are happening:

Strangers have taken her house,
They have stolen her kitchen,
They have put her in a cold bed.

4

It is summer. The singing grows urgent.
Twice a week, sometimes more,
I am called from sleep to walk in the night
And think of death.

I have been to the graveyard.
I have seen Uncle William's name
Written in stone.

I snap off the flashlight
And come in from the darkness under the trees
To the bedroom. Aunt Elsie is waiting.
I lean close to the pink ear.

5

Maybe this is what love is,
And always will be, all my life.

Whispering,
I give her an inch of hope

To bite on, like a bullet.

Farm Country

I have sharpened my knives, I have
Put on the heavy apron.

Maybe you think life is chicken soup, served
In blue willow-pattern bowls.

I have put on my boots and opened
The kitchen door and stepped out

Into the sunshine. I have crossed the lawn,
I have entered

The hen house.

Creeks

The dwindled creeks of summer,
Unremarkable except,
Down pasture, through woodlot,
They are so many
And keep such a pure sound
In each roiling thread,
Trickle past the knees of trees,
Dropped leaves, salamanders,
Each one scrubbing and cooling
The pebbles of its bed.

My back to hickory, I sit
Hours in the damp wood, listening.
It never ebbs.
Its music is the shelf for other sounds:
Birds, wind in the leaves, some tumbled stones.
After awhile
I forget things, as I have forgotten time.
Death, love, ambition—the things that drive
Like pumps in the big rivers.

                    My heart
Is quieted, at rest. I scarcely feel it.
Little rivers, running everywhere,
Have blunted the knife. Cool, cool,
They wash above the bones.

Roses

The look on her face in a dream
Stayed with me all day
Like a promise I had failed.

Not that I had made any—
Not that I could remember—
But she was looking into the north

Where nothing lives but white clouds
Of crying birds, like bits of snow.
And the grass on which she was standing,

And the roses thick on the fences
Were soft and bright, able to renew themselves
As a woman, finally, cannot do.

Winter in the Country

The terror of the country
Is not the easy death,
The fall of hawks out hunting
Across the musical earth,

Nor yet the useless borning
In every leafy den.
The terror is that nothing
Laments the narrow span.

Beasts of all marvelous feature,
Of vibrant hoof and wing,
Watch the white hands of winter
Undoing everything,

And do not cry or argue.
The starvlings of the day
Never dreamt of better.
Nibbling, they fall away.

The terror of the country
Is prey and hawk together,
Still flying, both exhausted,
In the blue sack of weather.

The Family

The dark things of the wood
Are coming from their caves,
Flexing muscle.

They browse the orchard,
Nibble the sea of grasses
Around our yellow rooms,

Scarcely looking in
To see what we are doing
And if they still know us.

We hear them, or think we do:
The muzzle lapping moonlight,
The tooth in the apple.

Put another log on the fire;
Mozart, again, on the turntable.
Still there is a sorrow

With us in the room.
We remember the cave.
In our dreams we go back

Or they come to visit.
They also like music.
We eat leaves together.

They are our brothers.
They are the family
We have run away from.

Ice

My father spent his last winter
Making ice-grips for shoes

Out of strips of inner tube and scrap metal.
(A device which slips over the instep

And holds under the shoe
A section of roughened metal, it allows you to walk

Without fear of falling
Anywhere on ice or snow.) My father

Should not have been doing
All that close work

In the drafty workshop, but as though
He sensed travel at the edge of his mind,

He would not be stopped. My mother
Wore them, and my aunt, and my cousins.

He wrapped and mailed
A dozen pairs to me, in the easy snows

Of Massachusetts, and a dozen
To my sister, in California.

Later we learned how he'd given them away
To the neighbors, an old man

Appearing with cold blue cheeks at every door.
No one refused him,

For plainly the giving was an asking,
A petition to be welcomed and useful—

Or maybe, who knows, the seed of a desire
Not to be sent alone out over the black ice.

Now the house seems neater: books,
Half-read, set back on the shelves;

Unfinished projects put away.
This spring

Mother writes to me: I am cleaning the workshop
And I have found

So many pairs of the ice-grips,
Cartons and suitcases stuffed full,

More than we can ever use.
What shall I do? And I see myself

Alone in that house with nothing
But darkly gleaming cliffs of ice, the sense

Of distant explosions,
Blindness as I look for my coat—

And I write back: Mother, please
Save everything.

Clam Man

He shuffles, and his face is white and lazy.
Some say he's crazy.
He sells clams

Door to door through town.
Once I was sound asleep but he banged at the glass
And woke me. "Want to buy

Some clams?" he shouted, staring
Not at me but into the house beyond.
"No," I said, ashamed
But frightened, and wished him away.

And he disappeared,
Banging the pail as he went
To scare the little breathers in their shells.

Bailing the Boat

In Ohio we did not have boats, we had horses.
And our talk was all of harness and barns,
Rubbing down and shoveling out,
Cooling off, checking bit and buckle,
The trim of the hoof, the look in the new colt's eye.

Well, we change, but we do not change much.

Done with bailing, I stow the gear
And cast off.
Snorting, the engine churns and comes alive!

And with arched neck she steps out over the water.

Crows

From a single grain they have multiplied.
When you look in the eyes of one
you have seen them all.

At the edges of highways
they pick at limp things.
They are anything but refined.

Or they fly out over the corn
like pellets of black fire,
like overlords.

Crow is crow, you say.
What else is there to say?
Drive down any road,

take a train or an airplane
across the world, leave
your old life behind,

die and be born again—
wherever you arrive
they'll be there first,

glossy and rowdy
and indistinguishable.
The deep muscle of the world.

The Rabbit

Scatterghost,
it can't float away.
And the rain, everybody's brother,
won't help. And the wind all these days
flying like ten crazy sisters everywhere
can't seem to do a thing. No one but me,
and my hands like fire,
to lift him to a last burrow. I wait

days, while the body opens and begins
to boil. I remember

the leaping in the moonlight, and can't touch it,
wanting it miraculously to heal
and spring up
joyful. But finally

I do. And the day after I've shoveled
the earth over, in a field nearby

I find a small bird's nest lined pale
and silvery and the chicks—

are you listening, death?—warm in the rabbit's fur.

Three Poems for James Wright

1. Hearing of Your Illness

I went out
from the news of your illness
like a broken bone.

I spoke your name
to the sickle moon and saw her white wing
fall back toward the blackness, but she
rowed deep past that hesitation, and
kept rising.

Then I went down
to a black creek and alder grove
that is Ohio like nothing else is
and told them. There was an owl there,
sick of its hunger but still
trapped in it, unable to be anything else.
And the creek
tippled on down over some dark rocks
and the alders
breathed fast in their red blossoms.

Then I lay down in a rank and spring-sweet field.
Weeds sprouting in the darkness, and some
small creatures rustling about, living their lives
as they do, moment by moment.

I felt better, telling them about you.
They know what pain is, and they knew you,
and they would have stopped too, as I

was longing to do, everything, the hunger
and the flowing.

That they could not—
merely loved you and waited
to take you back

as a stone,
as a small quick Ohio creek,
as the beautiful pulse of everything,
meanwhile not missing one shred of their own

assignments of song
and muscle—
was what I learned there, so I

got up finally, with a grief
worthy of you, and went home.

2. *Early Morning in Ohio*

A late snowfall.
In the white morning the trains
whistle and bang in the freightyard,
shifting track, getting ready
to get on with it, to roll out
into the country again, to get
far away from here and closer
to somewhere else.

A mile away, leaving the house, I hear them
and stop, astonished.

Of course. I thought they would stop
when you did. I thought you'd never sicken
anyway, or, if you did, Ohio
would fall down too, barn
by bright barn, into

hillsides of pain: torn boards,
bent nails, shattered
windows. My old dog

who doesn't know yet he is only mortal
bounds limping away
through the weeds, and I don't do
anything to stop him.

I remember
what you said.

And think how somewhere in Tuscany
a small spider might even now
be stepping forth, testing
the silks of her web, the morning air,
the possibilities; maybe even, who knows,
singing a tiny song.

And if the whistling of the trains drags through me
like wire, well, I can hurt can't I? The white fields
burn or my eyes swim, whichever; anyway I whistle
to the old dog and when he comes finally

I fall to my knees in the glittering snow, I throw
my arms around him.

3. The Rose

I had a red rose to send you,
but it reeked of occasion, I thought,
so I didn't. Anyway
it was the time
the willows do what they do
every spring, so I cut some
down by a dark Ohio creek and was ready
to mail them to you when the news came
that nothing
could come to you
in time
anymore
ever.

I put down the phone
and I thought I saw, on the floor of the room, suddenly,
a large box,
and I knew, the next thing I had to do,
was lift it
and I didn't know if I could.

Well, I did.
But don't call it anything
but what it was—the voice
of a small bird singing inside, Lord,
how it sang, and kept singing!
how it keeps singing!

in its deep
and miraculous
composure.

At Blackwater Pond

At Blackwater Pond the tossed waters have settled
after a night of rain.
I dip my cupped hands. I drink
a long time. It tastes
like stone, leaves, fire. It falls cold
into my body, waking the bones. I hear them
deep inside me, whispering
oh what is that beautiful thing
that just happened?

FROM

The River Styx, Ohio

and Other Poems

——  ——

(1 9 7 2)

Hattie Bloom

She was, Grandfather said, *a fly-by-night,*
And did just what you'd guess her kind would do!
Listening behind the door, I thought of Hattie,
Who'd sailed the town trailing her silks like wings
And seemed to me as elegant and pale
As any night bird cruising in its feathers.
She'd made my uncle wild, that much I knew.
Though he was grown, he wept; though he was strong,
She taught him what it was to want and fail.

True to her kind! Grandfather said, and sneered.
A fly-by-night! Come to your senses, boy!
But it was months before my uncle turned
Back to the world, before his eyes grew mild;
And it was years before he loved again.
And what was I to think of such conclusions—
Pressed to the door, a small and curious child
Eavesdropping on the terrifying world
Of sons and fathers talking of their women?

I knew that Hattie Bloom had run away
The night before, gone like a gust of wind
On the night train, her perfumes like a veil
Left on the platform; and I knew somehow
The kind of life she lived—yet understood
That love, which made my gentle uncle wild,
Might also change a painted girl to gold.
The dream that smiled and trailed its silken wing
Was what my uncle grieved for; and I thought
The truth of love was that in truth, for him,
Lost Hattie Bloom became that perfect thing.

Spring in the Classroom

Elbows on dry books, we dreamed
Past Miss Willow Bangs, and lessons, and windows,
To catch all day glimpses and guesses of the greening
    woodlot,
Its secrets and increases,
Its hidden nests and kind.
And what warmed in us was no book-learning,
But the old mud blood murmuring,
Loosening like petals from bone sleep.
So spring surrounded the classroom, and we suffered to be
    kept indoors,
Droned through lessons, carved when we could with
    jackknives
Our pulsing initials into the desks, and grew
Angry to be held so, without pity and beyond reason,
By Miss Willow Bangs, her eyes two stones behind glass,
Her legs thick, her heart
In love with pencils and arithmetic.

So it went—one gorgeous day lost after another
While we sat like captives and breathed the chalky air
And the leaves thickened and birds called
From the edge of the world—till it grew easy to hate,
To plot mutiny, even murder. Oh, we had her in chains,
We had her hanged and cold, in our longing to be gone!
And then one day, Miss Willow Bangs, we saw you
As we ran wild in our three o'clock escape
Past the abandoned swings; you were leaning
All furry and blooming against the old brick wall
In the Art Teacher's arms.

Alex

Where is Alex, keeper of horses?
Nobody knows.
He lived all year in the broken barn,
Dry summer stashed above the eaves.
Now that he's gone, who grieves, who can,
For Alex of the tangled beard?
The soiled old man,
He chased my brother once,
Waving a rusty gun,
And he had hungry eyes
For money and the bottle.

Last week the town officials
Came in their gleaming trucks
And tore his old barn down,
And the last horse was sold,
And he wasn't anywhere.
Well, maybe he's in the madhouse,
And maybe he's sleeping it off
Down at the edge of town,
Sprawled in a weedy bed,
Dreaming of horses and leather.

And maybe, with luck, he's dead.

Learning About the Indians

He danced in feathers, with paint across his nose.
Thump, thump went the drum, and bumped our blood,
And sent a strange vibration through the mind.
White Eagle, he was called, or Mr. White,

And he strutted for money now, in schoolrooms built
On Ohio's plains, surrounded by the graves
Of all of our fathers, but more of his than ours.
Our teachers called it Extracurricular.

We called it fun. And as for Mr. White,
Changed back to a shabby salesman's suit, he called it
Nothing at all as he packed his drums, and drove,
Tires screeching, out of the schoolyard into the night.

Night Flight

Traveling at thirty thousand feet, we see
How much of earth still lies in wilderness,
Till terminals occur like miracles
To civilize the paralyzing dark.

Buckled for landing to a tilting chair,
I think: if miracle or accident
Should send us on across the upper air,
How many miles, or nights, or years to go
Before the mind, with its huge ego paling,
Before the heart, all expectation spent,
Should read the meaning of the scene below?

But now already the loved ones gather
Under the dome of welcome, as we glide
Over the final jutting mountainside,
Across the suburbs tangled in their lights,

And settled softly on the earth once more
Rise in the fierce assumption of our lives—
Discarding smoothly, as we disembark,
All thoughts that held us wiser for a moment
Up there alone, in the impartial dark.

Anne

The daughter is mad, and so
I wonder what she will do.
But she holds her saucer softly
And sips, as people do,
From moment to moment making
Comments of rain and sun,
Till I feel my own heart shaking—
Till I am the frightened one.
O Anne, sweet Anne, brave Anne,
What did I think to see?
The rumors of the village
Have painted you savagely.
I thought you would come in anger—
A knife beneath your skirt.
I did not think to see a face
So peaceful, and so hurt.
I know the trouble is there,
Under your little frown;
But when you slowly lift your cup
And when you set it down,
I feel my heart go wild, Anne,
I feel my heart go wild.
I know a hundred children,
But never before a child
Hiding so deep a trouble
Or wanting so much to please,
Or tending so desperately all
The small civilities.

Answers

If I envy anyone it must be
My grandmother in a long ago
Green summer, who hurried
Between kitchen and orchard on small
Uneducated feet, and took easily
All shining fruits into her eager hands.

That summer I hurried too, wakened
To books and music and circling philosophies.
I sat in the kitchen sorting through volumes of answers
That could not solve the mystery of the trees.

My grandmother stood among her kettles and ladles.
Smiling, in faulty grammar,
She praised my fortune and urged my lofty career.
So to please her I studied—but I will remember always
How she poured confusion out, how she cooled and labeled
All the wild sauces of the brimming year.

The Esquimos Have No Word for "War"

Trying to explain it to them
Leaves one feeling ridiculous and obscene.
Their houses, like white bowls,
Sit on a prairie of ancient snowfalls
Caught beyond thaw or the swift changes
Of night and day.
They listen politely, and stride away

With spears and sleds and barking dogs
To hunt for food. The women wait
Chewing on skins or singing songs,
Knowing that they have hours to spend,
That the luck of the hunter is often late.

Later, by fires and boiling bones
In steaming kettles, they welcome me,
Far kin, pale brother,
To share what they have in a hungry time
In a difficult land. While I talk on
Of the southern kingdoms, cannon, armies,
Shifting alliances, airplanes, power,
They chew their bones, and smile at one another.

Encounter

I lift the small brown mouse
Out of the path and hold him.
He has no more to say,
No lilt of feet to run on.
He's cold, still soft, but idle.
As though he were a stone
I launch him from my hand;
His body falls away
Into the shadowed wood
Where the crackling leaves rain down,
Where the year is mostly over.
"Poor creature," I might say,
But what's the use of that.
The clock in him is broken.
And as for ceremony,
Already the leaves have swirled
Over, the wind has spoken.

Magellan

Like Magellan, let us find our islands
To die in, far from home, from anywhere
Familiar. Let us risk the wildest places,
Lest we go down in comfort, and despair.

For years we have labored over common roads,
Dreaming of ships that sail into the night.
Let us be heroes, or, if that's not in us,
Let us find men to follow, honor-bright.

For what is life but reaching for an answer?
And what is death but a refusal to grow?
Magellan had a dream he had to follow.
The sea was big, his ships were awkward, slow.

And when the fever would not set him free,
To his thin crew, "Sail on, sail on!" he cried.
And so they did, carried the frail dream homeward.
And thus Magellan lives, although he died.

Going to Walden

It isn't very far as highways lie.
I might be back by nightfall, having seen
The rough pines, and the stones, and the clear water.
Friends argue that I might be wiser for it.
They do not hear that far-off Yankee whisper:
How dull we grow from hurrying here and there!

Many have gone, and think me half a fool
To miss a day away in the cool country.
Maybe. But in a book I read and cherish,
Going to Walden is not so easy a thing
As a green visit. It is the slow and difficult
Trick of living, and finding it where you are.

The River Styx, Ohio

We drove through October, Grandmother pointing at cows;
Mother, bifocaled, squinting at maps for a crossroad.
We came instead to the River Styx, Ohio.

Dead leaves fell ruffling like an ugly lace
Down the brown hillsides, past some empty buildings.
We left the car and wandered through a field,
Three ladies pausing in indifferent space.

Some cows drank from a creek, and lurched away.
Whoever named the place learned the hard lesson,
I'd guess, without much fanfare or delay.
Farms to both sides shook, bankrupt, in the wind.

We hope for magic; mystery endures.
We look for freedom, but the measure's set.
There was a graveyard, but we saw no people.
We went back to the car.

Dim with arthritis, time, the muddied seasons,
Grandmother poised in the back seat again,
Counting the cows. My mother's tightening fingers
Scratched at the roads that would take us home. On the wheel
I tensed my knuckles, felt the first stab of pain.

FROM

No Voyage
and Other Poems

———— ❦ ————

(1 9 6 3   a n d   1 9 6 5)

No Voyage

I wake earlier, now that the birds have come
And sing in the unfailing trees.
On a cot by an open window
I lie like land used up, while spring unfolds.

Now of all voyagers I remember, who among them
Did not board ship with grief among their maps?—
Till it seemed men never go somewhere, they only leave
Wherever they are, when the dying begins.

For myself, I find my wanting life
Implores no novelty and no disguise of distance;
Where, in what country, might I put down these thoughts,
Who still am citizen of this fallen city?

On a cot by an open window, I lie and remember
While the birds in the trees sing of the circle of time.
Let the dying go on, and let me, if I can,
Inherit from disaster before I move.

O, I go to see the great ships ride from harbor,
And my wounds leap with impatience; yet I turn back
To sort the weeping ruins of my house:
Here or nowhere I will make peace with the fact.

The House

Because we lived our several lives
Caught up within the spells of love,
Because we always had to run
Through the enormous yards of day
To do all that we hoped to do,
We did not hear, beneath our lives,
The old walls falling out of true,
Foundations shifting in the dark.
When seedlings blossomed in the eaves,
When branches scratched upon the door
And rain came splashing through the halls,
We made our minor, brief repairs,
And sang upon the crumbling stairs
And danced upon the sodden floors.
For years we lived at peace, until
The rooms themselves began to blend
With time, and empty one by one,
At which we knew, with muted hearts,
That nothing further could be done,
And so rose up, and went away,
Inheritors of breath and love,
Bound to that final black estate
No child can mend or trade away.

Beyond the Snow Belt

Over the local stations, one by one,
Announcers list disasters like dark poems
That always happen in the skull of winter.
But once again the storm has passed us by:
Lovely and moderate, the snow lies down
While shouting children hurry back to play,
And scarved and smiling citizens once more
Sweep down their easy paths of pride and welcome.

And what else might we do? Let us be truthful.
Two counties north the storm has taken lives.
Two counties north, to us, is far away,—
A land of trees, a wing upon a map,
A wild place never visited,—so we
Forget with ease each far mortality.

Peacefully from our frozen yards we watch
Our children running on the mild white hills.
This is the landscape that we understand,—
And till the principle of things takes root,
How shall examples move us from our calm?
I do not say that it is not a fault.
I only say, except as we have loved,
All news arrives as from a distant land.

A Letter from Home

She sends me news of bluejays, frost,
Of stars and now the harvest moon
That rides above the stricken hills.
Lightly, she speaks of cold, of pain,
And lists what is already lost.
Here where my life seems hard and slow,
I read of glowing melons piled
Beside the door, and baskets filled
With fennel, rosemary and dill,
While all she could not gather in
Or hide in leaves, grows black and falls.
Here where my life seems hard and strange,
I read her wild excitement when
Stars climb, frost comes, and bluejays sing.
The broken year will make no change
Upon her wise and whirling heart;—
She knows how people always plan
To live their lives, and never do.
She will not tell me if she cries.

I touch the crosses by her name;
I fold the pages as I rise,
And tip the envelope, from which
Drift scraps of borage, woodbine, rue.

A Dream of Trees

There is a thing in me that dreamed of trees,
A quiet house, some green and modest acres
A little way from every troubling town,
A little way from factories, schools, laments.
I would have time, I thought, and time to spare,
With only streams and birds for company,
To build out of my life a few wild stanzas.
And then it came to me, that so was death,
A little way away from everywhere.

There is a thing in me still dreams of trees.
But let it go. Homesick for moderation,
Half the world's artists shrink or fall away.
If any find solution, let him tell it.
Meanwhile I bend my heart toward lamentation
Where, as the times implore our true involvement,
The blades of every crisis point the way.

I would it were not so, but so it is.
Who ever made music of a mild day?

The Murderer's House

Now small boys come to stare across the garden
Where flowers cast their petals day by day
Over the ground, and search the wind for winter,
And no one comes to chase the boys away.
This is a house of dark and mumbled fame.

Driving along at night, sometimes I've seen
A thin light burning deep within the rooms,
And thought how when the violent pass, how few
They leave to shed their tears upon the scene.

This is our failure, that in all the world
Only the stricken have learned how to grieve.
Safe in our cars, we pause along the highway
As one by one the leveling seasons fall;
And one by one we drive away, rejoicing
In such a distance as could strike us all.

Being Country Bred

Being country bred, I am at ease in darkness;
Like everything that thrives
In fields beyond the city's keep, I own
Five wooden senses, and a sixth like water.

These things I know
Before they set their mark upon the earth:
Chinook and snow,
Mornings of frost in the well, of birth in the barns.

Sweet world,
Think not to confuse me with poems or love beginning
Without a sign or sound:
Here at the edge of rivers hung with ice
Spring is still miles away, and yet I wake
Throughout the dark, listen, and throb with all
Her summoning explosions underground.

The Swimming Lesson

Feeling the icy kick, the endless waves
Reaching around my life, I moved my arms
And coughed, and in the end saw land.

Somebody, I suppose,
Remembering the medieval maxim,
Had tossed me in,
Had wanted me to learn to swim,

Not knowing that none of us, who ever came back
From that long lonely fall and frenzied rising,
Ever learned anything at all
About swimming, but only
How to put off, one by one,
Dreams and pity, love and grace,—
How to survive in any place.

Morning in a New Land

In trees still dripping night some nameless birds
Woke, shook out their arrowy wings, and sang,
Slowly, like finches sifting through a dream.
The pink sun fell, like glass, into the fields.
Two chestnuts, and a dapple gray,
Their shoulders wet with light, their dark hair streaming,
Climbed the hill. The last mist fell away,

And under the trees, beyond time's brittle drift,
I stood like Adam in his lonely garden
On that first morning, shaken out of sleep,
Rubbing his eyes, listening, parting the leaves,
Like tissue on some vast, incredible gift.

Swans on the River Ayr

Under the cobbled bridge the white swans float,
Slow in their perilous pride. Once long ago,
Led as a child along some Sunday lake,
I met these great birds, dabbling the stagnant shore.
We fed them bread from paper bags. They came,
Dipping their heads to take the stale slices
Out of our hands. Look! said the grownups, but
The child wept and flung the treacherous loaf.
Swans in a dream had no such docile eyes,
No humble beaks to touch a child's fingers.

In Ayr I linger on the cobbled bridge
And watch the birds. I will not tamper with them,
These ailing spirits clipped to live in cities
Whom we have tamed and made as sad as geese.
All swans are only relics of those birds
Who sail the tideless waters of the mind;
Who traveled once the waters of the earth,
Infecting dreams, helping the child to grow;
And who for ages, seeing witless man
Deck the rocks with gifts to make them mild,
Sensed the disaster to their uncaught lives,
And streamed shoreward like a white armada
With heads reared back to strike and wings like knives.

The Return

The deed took all my heart.
I did not think of you,
Not till the thing was done.
I put my sword away,
And then no more the cold
And perfect fury ran
Along my narrow bones,
And then no more the black
And dripping corridors
Held anywhere the shape
That I had come to slay.
Then, for the first time,
I saw in the cave's belly
The dark and clotted webs,
The green and sucking pools,
The rank and crumbling walls,
The maze of passages.

And I thought then
Of the far earth,
Of the spring sun
And the slow wind,
And a young girl.
And I looked then
At the white thread.

Hunting the minotaur
I was no common man
And had no need of love.
I trailed the shining thread

Behind me, for a vow,
And did not think of you.
It lay there, like a sign,
Coiled on the bull's great hoof
And back into the world.
Half blind with weariness
I touched the thread and wept.
O, it was frail as air.

And I turned then
With the white spool
Through the cold rocks,
Through the black rocks,
Through the long webs,
And the mist fell,
And the webs clung,
And the rocks tumbled,
And the earth shook.

And the thread held.

On Winter's Margin

On winter's margin, see the small birds now
With half-forged memories come flocking home
To gardens famous for their charity.
The green globe's broken; vines like tangled veins
Hang at the entrance to the silent wood.

With half a loaf, I am the prince of crumbs;
By time snow's down, the birds amassed will sing
Like children for their sire to walk abroad!
But what I love, is the gray stubborn hawk
Who floats alone beyond the frozen vines;
And what I dream of are the patient deer
Who stand on legs like reeds and drink the wind;—

They are what saves the world: who choose to grow
Thin to a starting point beyond this squalor.

My thanks to the editors of the following magazines, in which poems from the first section of this book have previously appeared:

Poetry (Rain, The Waterfall, This Morning Again It Was in the Dusty Pines), *The Virginia Quarterly Review* (Spring Azures, When Death Comes, A Bitterness), *Cream City Review* (Picking Blueberries, Austerlitz, New York, 1957), *Country Journal* (Her Grave, Peonies, Goldfinches, Morning), *Harvard Magazine* (Goldenrod), *The Southern Review* (Marengo; Field Near Linden, Alabama; Whelks), *Sierra* (Gannets), *Paris Review* (Alligator Poem, The Snowshoe Hare), *Wigwag* (Hawk), *Amicus* (Rice), *Kenyon Review* (Poppies), *The New Virginia Review* (A Certain Sharpness in the Morning Air, Water Snake, The Sun), *Wilderness* (Winter; Lonely, White Fields), *Atlantic* (White Flowers).

Poems from *House of Light* by Mary Oliver, copyright © 1990 by Mary Oliver. Reprinted by permission of Beacon Press.

Poems from *Dream Work* by Mary Oliver, copyright © 1986 by Mary Oliver. Reprinted by permission of the Atlantic Monthly Press.

Poems from *American Primitive* by Mary Oliver, copyright © 1978, 1979, 1980, 1981, 1982, 1983 by Mary Oliver. Reprinted by permission of Little, Brown and Company.

Poems from *Twelve Moons* by Mary Oliver, copyright © 1972, 1973, 1974, 1976, 1977, 1978, 1979 by Mary Oliver. Reprinted by permission of Little, Brown and Company.

Poems from *The Night Traveler* (published by Bits Press), *Sleeping in the Forest* (published by *The Ohio Review*), and five poems not previously included in any volume, by Mary Oliver, copyright © 1973, 1974, 1975, 1976, 1977, 1978, 1979, 1980, 1982 by Mary Oliver. Reprinted by permission of the author.

Poems from *The River Styx, Ohio and Other Poems* (published by Harcourt, Brace Jovanovich) by Mary Oliver, copyright © 1965, 1966, 1967, 1968, 1969, 1970, 1971, 1972 by Mary Oliver. Reprinted by permission of the author.

Poems from *No Voyage and Other Poems* (published by J. M. Dent and Sons, Ltd., London, in 1963; published by Houghton Mifflin in 1965) by Mary Oliver, copyright © 1959, 1960, 1961, 1962, 1963, 1964, 1965 by Mary Oliver. Reprinted by permission of the author.